HANG LOOSE, MOTHER GOOSE!

The Ultimate Nursery Rhyme Resource Guide

by dayle m timmons

Fearon Teacher Aids

**Lovingly dedicated
to all the little stars who have "twinkled" in my life
and
to Wesley and Courtney, "Star Light, Star Bright"
to Jimmy, "the first star" and the brightest star in my universe**

"Wish I may, wish I might, have this wish I wish tonight . . ."
To Susan Eddy, who made all my wishes come true . . .

With heartfelt thanks to Kerry Rogers, the "queen of hearts,"
who read each page of this manuscript and whose many creative suggestions
are included.

For continuing to sparkle in my life with ideas and support, my deep appreciation to
Mary Pat Byrnes, Kathy Grimm, Tish Hubard, Donna Kellam, Joy Mack, Sandy Price,
Michele Palmer, Cindy Tebbetts, Kathy Trukula, and Lauren Werch. Also special thanks to
Ann Winfree and the entire staff of the Children's Library of the Beach Branch of the
Jacksonville Public Library.

Editor: Susan Eddy

Illustrations: Olivia Cole

Cover and inside design: Robert Dobaczewski

Cover illustration: Judith Moffatt

Fearon Teacher Aids
An Imprint of Modern Curriculum
A Division of Simon & Schuster
299 Jefferson Road, P.O. Box 480
Parsippany, NJ 07054-0480

1 2 3 4 5 6 7 8 9 MAL 01 00 99 98 97

Contents

Why Nursery Rhymes?

Every generation of parents recites and sings to their children. And, as children grow, the most vivid and exciting of these rhymes and lullabies remain in children's memories and are taught to their own children. In this way, much like the folk tales of our oral tradition, some nursery rhymes have survived for hundreds of years, and an exemplary set of Mother Goose poems, known as nursery rhymes, has come down to us—sifted through generations of children. They are the ideal first literature for young children.

A child's ability to recite nursery rhymes in kindergarten is one of the best indicators of how well he or she will read. Because families are so busy today, many children come to school without the nurturing experience of sitting in the lap of a loving grown-up and committing nursery rhymes to memory. So it is often necessary for preschoolers and kindergartners to be introduced to these timeless jewels as part of their formal education. Even the child who comes to your class familiar with the rhymes will never tire of hearing them over and over.

Nursery rhymes are so perfect because they

* appeal to the humor level of young children

* have rhythm and rhyme

* have colorful characters

* provide a variety of subject matter

* have a simple story line

* can be recited over and over without boredom

* provide opportunities for drama

* are so easy to remember

* are abundantly available

* are familiar to parents

Nursery rhymes are the perfect beginning for the first grader, whose familiarity with the rhymes provides the base for teaching language conventions, phonetic skills, creative dramatics, and so on. The rhymes lend themselves beautifully to artistic reproductions and creative innovations.

The vast array of illustrated collections of nursery rhymes speaks to the sacred place that Mother Goose holds in our culture. There are over 130 nursery-rhyme collections currently in print—many beautifully illustrated by some of our finest children's book illustrators. Don't pass up this treasure trove of poetry and art—among the finest our heritage has to offer.

How to Use This Book

Hang Loose, Mother Goose is not a curriculum guide. No teacher is meant to use every single idea contained in each unit. Instead, it is a resource book—an idea book—from which to select ideas that meet your needs and pique your fancy.

The range of activities provided for each of the eight thematic units stretches across the curriculum from the beginner to the most advanced student. Each unit provides more than enough suggestions to meet your specific goals and objectives. You are encouraged to merge ideas in this book with your own creativity and knowledge of skill development and to adapt and change any suggestion to meet your individual needs.

The book is arranged to accomplish this in a variety of ways. Individual rhymes are self-contained and can stand alone. In other words, "Little Bo Peep" is its own miniunit with its own activities. However, rhymes may also be used in the context of a larger theme. For example, four rhymes are used to teach the theme "Sheep and Lambs" with culminating activities to bring each of the rhymes together into a thematic context (Sheep and Lamb Activities). These culminating activities can also be pulled out and used with any of the individual rhymes from the unit.

Teachers will use the eight thematic units in a variety of ways.

- ❋ Some teachers will spend two months teaching as many of the rhymes as possible—a unit each week. They will use the rhymes as their literature base for a whole-language program—a program based on skill development!

- ❋ Other teachers will pick and choose some of the more popular rhymes, such as Humpty Dumpty, Jack and Jill, Hey Diddle Diddle, or Little Miss Muffet. They will only be interested in the whole-language aspect of the rhymes, spending two to three weeks on an entire unit.

- ❋ Still others will want to incorporate appropriate rhymes into other units that they teach throughout the year (see *Other Thematic Links*).

No matter which of these paths you take up the mountain, you'll find that they all lead to the same destination—a love for the humor and rhythm of nursery rhymes! Enjoy wonderful memories of your childhood as you share with your class the love and warmth of all that is good about being young, free-spirited, and in love with life. Pass on to this new generation the timeless words of those who traveled this path before us. Soak in the sunshine that will sparkle in the eyes of your children as they laugh, play, reenact, and thoroughly enjoy every day of these units! They, in turn, will some day plant new seeds in a new generation of children, and you will truly have touched the future.

Get ready ... Mother Goose is on the loose!

MOON
AND
STAR
RHYMES

Hey Diddle Diddle
I See the Moon
Twinkle Twinkle Little Star
Star Light, Star Bright

Hey, diddle, diddle! The cat and the fiddle,
The cow jumped over the moon.
The little dog laughed to see such sport,
And the dish ran away with the spoon!

A traditional tune for this all-time favorite nursery rhyme, which has been called the "best-known nonsense verse in the language," can be found in Pamela Beall and Susan Nipp's *Wee Sing Nursery Rhymes and Lullabies* (Price, Stern & Sloan, 1985). *The Wee Sing* set comes with a cassette and sing-along book. It is easily found in most toy, book, or school-supply stores or can be ordered directly from Price, Stern & Sloan Publishers, Inc., 410 North La Cienega Boulevard, Los Angeles, CA 90048, 1-800-631-8571

Children will love Marilyn Janovitz's *Hey Diddle Diddle* (Hyperion, 1995) which tries to make sense of the nursery rhyme, and Moira Kemp's board book version of *Hey Diddle Diddle* (Dutton, 1991) with its delightful illustrations. Both books illustrate the rhyme line-by-line.

This is a favorite rhyme for acting out. Give each child an appropriate prop for playing the cat, cow, moon, dog, dish, and spoon. Or you may wish to photocopy the pictures on pages 268–272. You can thread these pictures on yarn for children to wear around their necks or staple them to tongue depressors for children to hold (consider sending these props home with the children). As the "audience" says the rhyme, the following actions take place on the appropriate lines. Children will want to repeat this drama over and over!

> The cat pretends to play the fiddle.
>
> The cow jumps over the moon.
>
> The little dog laughs (a favorite part!)
>
> The dish takes the spoon by the hand and they pretend to run away.

Make a reproduction of this rhyme using the scenes and props from above and an instant camera. Take a photograph of each line action (one photo of the cat with his fiddle, one photo of the cow jumping over the moon, one photo of the dog laughing, and one picture of the dish and the spoon holding hands). Glue each photograph to tagboard and write the appropriate line at the bottom. Laminate for durability and bind pages together into a big book. You may have to make several books in order to get every child in at least one picture.

Encourage volunteers to illustrate each of the four lines of the rhyme with markers or crayons for an original illustrated book. Or, for something different, have children use overhead pens to illustrate each line of the verse on a transparency. Children flash their transparencies on an overhead projector as they say the rhyme.

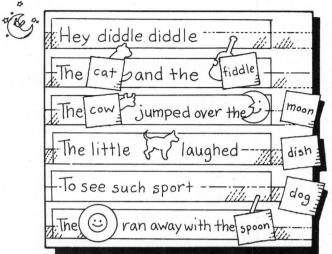

Write the rhyme on chart paper, replacing the words *cat*, *fiddle*, *cow*, *moon*, *dog*, *dish*, and *spoon* with pictures. Point to each word as you read the rhyme with the class. When you come to a picture, stop and have children say the appropriate word. Write each word on a sticky note and add these to the chart. Encourage children to match the words and pictures by sticking the word over the picture.

 Invite children to use washable markers on the laminated chart to circle two rhyming words, two words that are exactly alike, or three animal words; underline capital letters; make an X at the beginning of each line; circle nonsense words; and so on. Try to identify a new concept each day.

Hey, Diddle, Diddle

Hey, diddle, diddle,
The (cat) and the fiddle,
The (cow) jumped over the moon.
The little (dog) laughed to
  see such sport
And the dish ran away
  with the spoon!

 Photocopy, color, and laminate the nursery-rhyme illustration on page 7. Have children identify things that they see in the picture, making sure that they use the basic vocabulary of the rhyme. Draw lines from the identified nouns to written words. Review the main vocabulary from the rhyme each day. Children may use magnetic letters to spell out these words on a chalk or magnetic board.

 Explain to children that a fiddle is a violin. Invite someone to come in and play the violin for the children—both classical and country "fiddle" music if possible. Call your local symphony or high-school music director for suggestions. Perhaps your music teacher has a violin or recordings of violin music. If there is a Suzuki program nearby, those students will be able to play many variations of "Twinkle Twinkle Little Star."

Have each child make an individual accordion-book of the rhyme. Accordion-fold a piece of tagboard into four sections for each book. Write one line of the rhyme at the bottom of each section and have children illustrate each line with markers, crayons, or precut construction-paper shapes of a cat, fiddle, moon, cow, dog, circle dish, and spoon. Ellison die-cuts work well for projects such as this one.

Hey, diddle, diddle, The cat and the fiddle,

The cow jumped over the moon.

The little dog laughed to see such sport,

And the dish ran away with the spoon!

Make a favorite-character graph. On the bottom or left-hand side of a piece of tagboard, place pictures of the main characters: cat with his fiddle, cow, dog, and the dish and spoon. Give each child a star cutout or small school photo to place in a row beside his or her favorite character. Discuss the graph. Encourage children to draw pictures of themselves with their favorite characters to display around the graph.

Have children trace circles and then cut moons from squares of yellow construction paper. Then have them glue their moons to sheets of black construction paper. Give each child a sheet of gummed stars to place in the night sky or have children cut their own stars with a star-shaped hole punch. Precut construction-paper cow shapes or look for cow stickers for children to place in the night sky jumping over the moon.

Favorite character

Designate something in your room, such as a large cardboard block, to be the "moon" and encourage children to jump over the moon. Or simply have children use a stencil to draw and cut out a moon from a piece of yellow construction paper. They can place this moon on the floor and jump over it.

 Give each child a yellow paper plate or a yellow construction-paper circle to symbolize a moon. Each child will also need a cow, either cut from paper or from a toy farm set. Practice position words and have children act out what you say using the moons and cows. For example, the cow jumped over the moon, the cow crawled under the moon, the cow played on the moon, the cow hid under the moon, the cow jumped up and down on the moon, the cow stood beside the moon, or the cow danced around the moon. You (and the children!) will think of others.

 Adapt a language chunk like "... and the cow jumped over the moon" to make a class book. Ask children if this line is real or make-believe. Could a cow really jump over the moon? Have children use yellow markers to draw moons (circles) and then add themselves jumping over the moon. Under each picture, write *(Child's name) jumped over the moon*. For a cover, write the title, "The Cow Jumped Over the Moon!" and draw a picture of the cow jumping over the moon. Laminate the pictures and bind together for a class book.

 Children will enjoy the fingerwiggle book *Hey Diddle Diddle* by Colin and Jacqui Hawkins (Candlewick Press, 1992). It has die-cut holes in each board page for children to put their fingers through and wiggle. In the illustration on the cover, children put their fingers through two holes and provide the legs for the dish that ran away with the spoon. Other rhymes included are "This Little Piggy" and "Little Miss Muffet."

 Children will enjoy James Marshall's board book *Hey Diddle Diddle* (Farrar Straus Giroux, 1979), which has an original second verse. After reading Marshall's verse, encourage children to write verses of their own. Provide a framework by having children fill in the blanks on page 12. Encourage children to illustrate any new rhymes that they write.

Hey diddle diddle

The_____ and the fiddle

The _____ jumped over the moon

The little _____ laughed to see such sport

And the _____ ran away with the spoon.

Or adapt the rhyme, using the names of children in the class.

Hey diddle diddle

Gabrielle with the fiddle

Daniel jumped over the moon

Mrs. Timmons laughed to see such sport

And Sarah ran away with the spoon.

Read Jim Aylesworth's *The Cat and the Fiddle and More* (Macmillan Children's Group, 1992) to the class. This delightful book has many whimsical rhymes that use the "Hey Diddle Diddle" format, such as "Hey trifle trifle" and "Hey sunny sunny." Each verse is illustrated. Work with the class to write more new verses. Discuss with children the lines that rhyme in the original poem so that they will have a structure for new verses. Read each new verse with the class and invite children to illustrate them. Display in the classroom and then bind into a class book.

Enjoy *The Little Dog Laughed* by Lucy Cousins (E.P. Dutton, 1989), a collection of 64 nursery rhymes with illustrations that resemble children's artwork. "Hey Diddle Diddle" is included. See if children have any idea why the author chose *The Little Dog Laughed* as her title!

"Hey Diddle Diddle" is part of almost every nursery-rhyme collection. Display several collections of nursery rhymes in your book center. Each day, flip through the illustrations of one book and ask children after turning each page, "Is this *Hey Diddle Diddle?*" Children will delight in identifying the verse from the illustrations. This exercise helps young children begin to see the importance of using illustrations to help them understand what they are reading.

 Charles A. Micucci's *A Little Night Music* (Morrow, 1989) is about a cat that plays the fiddle at night and eventually dances with the dog. Although this book is not based on the rhyme, some of the characters are similar. Discuss these similarities with the class and encourage children to write their own original adventures using nursery-rhyme characters.

I see the mo͞on and the mo͞on sees me.
God bless the mo͞on and God bless me.

Write this rhyme on chart paper and laminate. Choose letters or words from the rhyme and invite children to come up and mark the selected letters or words with a wipe-off marker. For example, circle the word *moon*, put a red rectangle around all of the e's, or draw a purple triangle around each period.

Chant this verse using a steady beat. Clap on the underlined words.

I see the <u>mo͞on</u> and the <u>mo͞on</u> sees <u>me</u>.

<u>God</u> bless the <u>mo͞on</u> and <u>God</u> bless <u>me</u>.

After children have mastered *clapping* the steady beat, have them suggest other ways to keep time, such as snapping fingers, hands over head-hands down, or tapping index fingers together.

Have each child illustrate the rhyme with a moon picture. First children draw faces on moons made from yellow paper plates or circles cut from yellow construction paper. The moons are glued to black or dark blue construction paper. Children may add foil gummed stars to the night sky. Then have each child draw a self-portrait on white construction paper, cut around the self-portrait, and glue it to the night picture. Display the pictures on a bulletin board or wall with the title, "I See the Moon and the Moon Sees Me."

 Read *I See the Moon and the Moon Sees Me* by Jonathan London (Viking, 1996) which is based on the first line of the rhyme ("I see the sun and the sun sees me . . ." and so on). This should give children ideas for new lines of their own, such as "I see the teacher and the teacher sees me. God bless the teacher and God bless me."

Illustrate ". . . and the moon sees me" by making paper-plate moon masks from yellow paper plates. Cut out the eye holes and have children finish the face with markers. Attach moon faces to tongue depressors and have children hold up the masks as they say the rhyme. Encourage them to make up verses on the spot by identifying things that they see through the moon-mask eyes. For example, "I see the window and the window sees me. God bless the window and God bless me."

 Write the replacement words on sticky notes to place over the original rhyme words on the laminated chart. Then read the new verses with the class. Have children illustrate each new verse. Add the new words to the bottoms of the pictures and bind these adaptations into a class book that will be read over and over.

I See the [teacher]

I see the m[teacher]
and the m[teacher] sees me
God bless the m[teacher]
and God bless me.

Write each line of the original verse on a sentence strip and cut the sentence strips into individual words. Arrange the words in a pocket chart following the sequence of the verse. Point to each word as you say the verse with the class. Then use the cut-up words to play a game. Have children cover their eyes while you turn one word over so that you see only the blank strip in the word's place. Have children guess what the word is. The child who guesses the word first gets to turn over the next word.

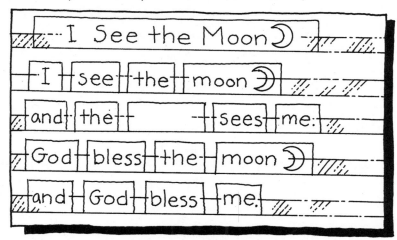

 After the words are cut up, put the words in alphabetical order or use the cut-up words as sight-word flash cards.

 Look for Helen Craig's *I See the Moon and the Moon Sees Me . . .* (Willa Perlman Books, 1992), a collection of traditional rhymes with whimsical illustrations.

 Serve Moon Pies for snack (available in any grocery store)—a piece of the "moon" between two pieces of the "night sky"! Encourage children to make up stories about how moon pies are made. Who fetches the pieces of moon? How do they get the pieces of night sky?

Share Shel Silverstein's poem "Moon Catchin' Net" from *A Light in the Attic* (HarperCollins, 1981). After reading the poem to the class, cut some star and moon shapes from sponges and fun foam to float in the water table. Add some nets and have children scoop up the stars and moons in aquarium nets.

Twinkle twinkle little star,
How I wonder what you are!
Up above the world so high,
Like a diamond in the sky,
Twinkle twinkle little star,
How I wonder what you are!

 Janet Messenger's *Twinkle Twinkle Little Star* (Macmillan, 1986) is a wonderful book to present to children as an introduction to this rhyme. This expanded version includes a battery that supplies power for a little twinkling light and a music chip. This small book will enthrall children.

A traditional tune for this rhyme (written by Mozart at the age of six!) can be found in Pamela Beall and Susan Nipp's *Wee Sing Nursery Rhymes and Lullabies* (Price, Stern & Sloan, 1985). The *Wee Sing* set comes with audio cassette and sing-along book. The series can be found in most toy, book, or school-supply stores or can be ordered directly from Price, Stern & Sloan Publishers, Inc., 410 North La Cienega Boulevard, Los Angeles, CA 90048, 1-800-631-8571. This particular version of the song includes several other verses.

The original "Twinkle Twinkle Little Star" was written in the 1880s by the poet Jane Taylor as a Christmas story entitled "The Star." Look for Jane Taylor's original verse in the following illustrated versions.

Twinkle Twinkle Little Star illustrated by Michael Hague (Scholastic, 1993).

Twinkle Twinkle Little Star (Morrow, 1992).

Twinkle Twinkle Little Star illustrated by Wendy Staw (Wishing Well Books, 1995).

Using the traditional tune, teach the following traditional hand motions to "Twinkle Twinkle Little Star."

Twinkle twinkle little star,	Flash fingers open and shut.
How I wonder what you are!	Hand on forehead, looking up.
Up above the world so high,	Point up to sky.
Like a diamond in the sky,	Make a diamond with your fingers by matching both thumbs and both index fingers.
Twinkle twinkle little star,	Flash fingers open and shut.
How I wonder what you are!	Hand on forehead, looking up.

Write this rhyme on chart paper and laminate. Choose letters or words from the rhyme and invite children to come up and mark the selected letters or words with a wipe-off marker. For example, circle the word *star*, put a red rectangle around all of the e's, or draw a green triangle around each period, or underline two sentences that match.

 Using the chart-paper rhyme, point to each word as you read the verse with the class. Make a pointer by hot-gluing a glittery star to the end of a dowel (these can sometimes be found ready-made as fairy princess wands, especially around Halloween). Leave the pointer out so that children will be encouraged to "read" this rhyme and others displayed in the room using the pointer all by themselves.

Help children make their own magic star wands. Roll a sheet of bond paper very tightly, starting in one corner. Roll on the diagonal and seal with a small piece of clear tape to hold the stick shape. Have children paint and glitter two star shapes. Staple the stars together with the wand in the middle. Or use paper star cutouts attached to tongue depressors. It's magic! Twinkle, twinkle . . . .

 Make magic star wand healthy snacks. Give each child a stalk of celery to fill with pimento cheese, cream cheese, or peanut butter. Use a small star-shaped cookie cutter to cut a star from sliced cheese for each child. Place the star at the end of the "wand." Make a wish!

 Consider purchasing some glow-in-the-dark stars to put on the ceiling of your bathroom or another area that can be darkened. Have children go in, shut the door, and watch the stars glow as they sing "Twinkle twinkle little star." Or sprinkle glitter on some star shapes and attach flat to the ceiling for a little daytime twinkle.

Put out star shapes to trace at the writing table (star-shaped cookie cutters and stencils) and black or white construction paper. Add glitter crayons or glow-in-the-dark crayons (available from Crayola in chubby size) for children to use to trace and color the stars. Lighter crayons show up better on black paper, but any color will show on white. Advise children to color inside each star heavily to create a glittering, glowing night sky. If they use glow-in-the-dark crayons, be sure to take the pictures into a darkened space and watch them glow. Look also for glow-in-the-dark books to share.

Make a bulletin board with the title "Twinkle Twinkle Little Star!" Include a star created by each child, cut out and decorated with glitter and sequins (these also make a great bulletin-board border), and photographs of the children playing in the room or self-portraits drawn by the children.

Cut star shapes from different colors of tagboard to use as color flashcards. Hold up the stars and have children identify each color. Adapt the predictable sequence from Eric Carle's *Brown Bear, Brown Bear* as you identify the colors. Hesitate before saying each color word so that children say them for you.

<u>Red</u> star, <u>red</u> star, What do you see?

I see a <u>green</u> star twinkling at me.

<u>Green</u> star, <u>green</u> star, What do you see?

I see a <u>blue</u> star twinkling at me.

Have children make their own "Red Star, Red Star" books by using cut or colored stars. Prepare photocopied pages with one line of the verse per page. Staple the pages together to make a book for each child. Children add the appropriately colored star to each page. Send the books home to be "read" to mom and dad!

" . . . like a diamond in the sky." Discuss this language chunk with the class. Show children how to draw diamond shapes.

 * Trace diamonds.

 * Make dot-to-dot diamonds.

 * Cut out diamond shapes of different sizes and colors to make a colorful collage.

 * Put out diamond shapes cut from heavy cardboard for children to use as stencils.

 * Make your own stencils by cutting diamond shapes out from the insides of large plastic lids. Children place these homemade stencils flat on pieces of paper and trace around the inside.

 * Look for diamond-shaped cookie cutters to add to play dough or to dip in paint and make prints on colored construction paper.

The exquisitely illustrated *Twinkle Twinkle Little Star* by Iza Trapani (Whispering Coyote Press, 1994) begins with the original rhyme and then adds new verses. This book is a must-have.

 For a wonderful twist to the original tune, look for the audio cassette *Shake It All About* (Walt Disney, 1992) and enjoy Little Richard's version of "Twinkle Twinkle Little Star." Children will love listening to this modern version of the song, which will have even your quietest child up and dancing!

Star light, star bright,
First star I see tonight,
Wish I may, wish I might
Have this wish I wish tonight.

Place a star somewhere in the room (a different place each day) during the time that you study this verse. The first child to find the star each morning and say the rhyme gets to give a treat to each member of the class (a single Starburst candy, for example).

Practice chanting this rhyme with children. Once they are very familiar with it, have children use motions to keep a steady beat (clapping, snapping fingers, hitting thighs) as you say the words. Bring out your rhythm instruments and have children keep the beat with bells and triangles. Do the bells sound like twinkling night stars?

Have children sit in a circle with you. When you lift your arm up high, children *shout* the rhyme. When you hold your arm in the middle, children say the rhyme in a *normal* tone. When you place your hand on the floor, children *whisper* the rhyme. Move your hand up and down as children follow your lead with their voices. Then choose a child to be the leader. This is a fun way to memorize the rhyme!

 Write this rhyme on chart paper and laminate. Choose letters or words from the rhyme and invite children to come up and mark the selected letters or words with a wipe-off marker. For example, they can circle the word *star*, circle rhyming words, or draw a square around capital letters.

 List words that rhyme in this poem (*light, bright, tonight*). Have children try out other consonants and blends to brainstorm a list of other words that end with *-ight*.

 Make a class wish book using sentence strips. Talk with children about things that people wish for. Share your own wishes as well. Have each child finish the sentence *(Child's name) wishes* _____ and write down the child's dictation. Give each child an index card on which to illustrate his or her wish. Glue the illustrations to the ends of the sentence strips. Add a cover sentence strip with the line "Wish I may, wish I might . . ." and invite children to decorate it with a star-shaped marker or rubber stamp. Punch a hole in the end of each sentence strip and bind together with a ring binder.

Have children make paper wishing stars decorated with glitter, sequins, foil paper, and other shiny beads and baubles. Add some gold, silver, or iridescent ribbons of different widths to the bottoms of a few stars to make shooting stars. Hang the stars from the ceiling with fishing line. As children find their stars in the "sky," they say the rhyme and make a wish.

 For some "star light, star bright," cut star shapes out of the middle of sheets of black or white construction paper. Cover one side of the construction paper with clear self-adhesive plastic and turn over to expose the sticky side. Cut pieces of colorful, shiny ribbon or construction paper squares to cover the exposed sticky star. After covering the sticky side, turn the paper over to see the colorful star. For translucent stars, cover the sticky part with small pieces of tissue paper and tape to a window to see the star shine.

 "Star bright!" Draw star and moon shapes on an overhead transparency. Place the overhead projector on the floor and project the star shapes onto a smooth wall. Leave out markers and colorful paper so that children can put their papers on the wall and trace the stars and moons using the outlines from the transparency. Then they can cut out the stars to make a class collage on a large sheet of black craft paper. Share Shel Silverstein's "Somebody Has To" from *A Light in the Attic* (HarperCollins, 1981)—a poem about someone having to shine the stars. Copy the poem and add to a bulletin-board display of moon and stars.

Read Karen Davis' *Star Light, Star Bright* (Simon & Schuster, 1993)— the delightful story of Louisa looking for a wishing star at night; also incorporates the rhyme.

Moon and Star Activities

  Make a listening tape for the class by recording moon-and-star rhymes from commercial tapes. Include traditional and modern versions, such as Little Richard's interpretation of "Twinkle Twinkle Little Star." Intermingle commercial selections with the class and individual children singing and reading the nursery rhymes.

  Use star or moon shapes to make number flashcards. Cut stars from tagboard or use sheets of star- or moon-shaped notepaper for each flashcard. Put one number on each colorful shape and flash the cards in order. Then say one of the moon-and-star rhymes while you mix up the numbers and flash them in random order. Leave the star flashcards out so that children can sequence them at their leisure. Use the flashcards to encourage more advanced students to make their own simple addition and subtraction problems. Make flashcards for alphabet letters and sight words, too.

  Cut stars from tagboard in three different sizes and colors for children to sort by size and then by color.

  Use the colored star cutouts to work on memory skills. Place four or five stars in front of children and ask them to identify the colors. Then have them hide their eyes and recite one of the moon-and-star rhymes while you take one of the stars away. Children uncover their eyes and guess which color is missing.

Cut 10 or 20 pieces of black tagboard about 5 in. by 8 in. (12.5 cm by 20 cm). Glue a yellow construction-paper moon (or look for moon-shaped die-cut note pads) to each card. Write a number on each moon and laminate. Collect "stars" that can be used as counters, such as small star-shaped erasers, large sequins, or plastic star-shaped beads. Children lay the moon cards out in numerical order and then count the appropriate number of "stars" onto each card. Challenge children to make addition problems from different-colored counters. For instance, if a child places three red stars, one blue star, and six yellow stars on the number 10 moon, encourage him or her to write an addition sentence reflecting this (3 + 1 + 6 = 10).

More mature students can use moon and star shapes for matching activities. Shapes may be cut from tagboard, or die-cut note pads can be used. For instance, children can match uppercase letters on moon cutouts to lowercase letters on star cutouts. Sets of moons and stars can be used for matching numerals to sets, numerals to number words, colors to color words, alphabet letters to pictures of initial consonant sounds, rhyming pictures, and so on.

Look for star-shaped snacks, such as SnackWells Cinnamon Graham Snacks or the star-shaped exotic fruit called carabolas. Make "star food" using star-shaped cookie cutters to cut cheese slices into star shapes, to make star-shaped toast, or to cut star-shaped Jigglers using the following recipe. Have children choose the number of stars that they want and then count them out. Or give each child the same number and practice some subtraction. "Eat one. How many do you have left?"

 Star Jigglers

     4 envelopes unflavored gelatin

     3 3-oz packages flavored gelatin

     4 cups boiling water

Mix boiling water with gelatins and stir until dissolved. Carefully pour onto a jelly-roll pan (cookie sheet with a rim). Chill until set. Invite children to cut the stiff gelatin into star shapes using a small star-shaped cookie cutter.

 After children have a star Jiggler, have them dictate five-senses poems following the outline below. Children might dictate to parent volunteers or to upper-grade "buddies." Mount the poems on star-shaped construction paper and display on a bulletin board with the title, "Where the Stars of Tomorrow Shine Today."

     Star Jigglers look _____.

     Star Jigglers taste _____.

     Star Jigglers feel _____.

     Star Jigglers smell _____.

     Star Jigglers sound _____.

Cut star shapes from tagboard for children to use as backgrounds for collages. Collect interesting things for children to glue to their stars, such as pompoms, beads, pipe cleaners, fabric, and felt cut into small shapes, broken crayons, ribbons, and so on. Or cover the stars with aluminum foil and look for baubles of silver and gold to glue to the stars (foil paper, sequins, beads, sparkly pipe cleaners, silver and gold ribbon of different widths, glitter). Glue the sparkly stars to a bulletin board covered with black or dark blue paper. Add the title, "Teach a Child to Touch a Star."

Add star- and circle-shaped cookie cutters to your play dough area so that children can make stars and moons. For a little added sparkle, sprinkle some gold, silver, or iridescent glitter into the play dough. Tell children it's magic star dust!

Have children use round and star-shaped cookie cutters to make a collage of shapes. Pour paint into plastic foam meat trays and put a cookie cutter in each tray. Children dip the cookie cutters into the paint and print the outlines on paper in any way they like. A little iridescent glitter may be added to the finished picture while the paint is still wet.

Look for metallic moon and star confetti (available with party supplies) to make a sparkling bottle to float in your water table. Fill a clear plastic bottle almost full of water and add a handful of confetti and a little glitter. Twist the top back on and hot glue around the closed top to keep children from emptying the bottle. Children will love turning the bottle back and forth and watching it float in the water table.

Sprinkle the rest of the metallic confetti in your sand table or simply use metallic glitter for a little "star dust" in your sand.

Collect star-shaped floating candles or star-shaped permanent plastic ice cubes to float in your water table. Or cut some stars from fun foam (a thin, pressed sponge that you can buy in sheets at most craft stores) to float. The fun foam also adheres to the sides of a water table. Add some small aquarium nets so children can enjoy catching the stars in the nets.

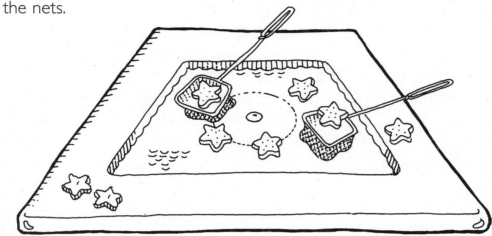

Have children make starry night pictures by using stencils to trace outlines of stars and a moon on white paper. They then fill in each outline with colored glue or glitter glue. When the glue is dry, children may paint the paper with thinned black tempera. The paint will adhere to the paper but not to the dried glue.

Children will enjoy fingerpainting with glitter fingerpaint (make your own by sprinkling dark blue or black fingerpaint with glitter). Explain to children that the glitter is the stars sparkling in the night sky.

Help children make star headbands by precutting stars in two or three different sizes from colorful construction paper. Give each child a sentence strip or construction-paper strip and have children glue on stars in any design they choose. Staple the strips to fit each child's head.

Fold a piece of construction paper into eight equal parts. Write a number in each section—higher numbers for more mature students. Have children place the appropriate number of stars into each section using a star-shaped rubber stamp, a star-shaped marker, or gummed stars.

Make number sticks by placing a number of gummed stars (or use a star-shaped marker) on several tongue depressors. Younger students can put the sticks in numerical order. More mature students can use them to make addition and subtraction problems.

 Design a bulletin board featuring the star theme. Look for fabric with a starry design. Cut enough fabric (use pinking shears) so that when you staple or pin it to the top of the bulletin board, it hangs to the bottom. Tie back the sides with colorful ribbon or fabric as you would for a window or stage curtain. For a title, use "Starring . . ." as if to say these children will star in your production this year! Add the subtitle, "Directed by (Mrs. Timmons)." Fill the bulletin board with photographs or pictures and star shapes cut by the children.

 More mature students will enjoy a field trip to a planetarium. After they return, have them draw simple line pictures with white crayon or chalk on black paper and add gummed stars at certain points of the drawing to make their own constellations. Have children name their original star formations.

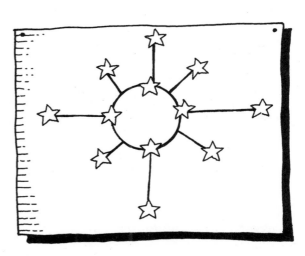

 Have an assortment of books at your book center featuring moon-and-star themes to give children ideas for their own stories and artistic endeavors. Read some of the books to the class each day, making sure to teach and discuss as you go. The following are only a few of the possibilities.

Asch, Frank. *Happy Birthday, Moon*. Simon & Schuster, 1982.

Berger, Barbara. *Grandfather Twilight*. Philomel, 1984.

Branley, Franklyn M. *The Sky Is Full of Stars*. HarperCollins, 1983.

Brown, Marcia. *Goodnight Moon*. Scholastic, 1993. (book with audio cassette)

Brown, Marcia. *Goodnight Moon Board Book*. HarperCollins, 1992.

Brown, Marcia. *The Goodnight Moon Room: A Pop-Up Book*. HarperCollins, 1985.

Brown, Marcia. *Goodnight Moon Bedtime Box*. HarperCollins, 1992.

Carle, Eric. *Draw Me a Star*. Philomel Books, 1992.

Carle, Eric. *Papa, Please Get the Moon for Me*. Picture Book Studios, 1986.

Carlstrom, Nancy White. *The Moon Came, Too*. Macmillan, 1987.

Conlon-McKenna, Marita. *Little Star*. Little Brown, 1993.

Dayrell, E. *Why the Sun and Moon Live in the Sky*. Houghton-Mifflin, 1990.

Duncan, Lois. *Birthday Moon*. Viking Children's Books, 1989.

Field, Susan. *The Sun, the Moon and the Silver Baboon*. HarperCollins, 1993.

George, Lonnie. *Star, Little Star*. Grosset and Dunlap, 1992.

Hines, Anne Grossnickle. *Moon's Wish*. Clarion, 1992.

Hort, Lenny. *How Many Stars in the Sky?* Morrow, 1991.

Ichikawa, Satomi. *Nora's Stars*. Philomel Books, 1989.

Murphy, Jill. *What Next, Baby Bear!* Dial, 1986.

Warlow, Aidan. *Start With Rhymes: Round the Moon*. Wright Group, 1988. (part of a six-book set of individual nursery-rhyme books)

Wright, Kit. *Tigerella*. Scholastic, 1994.

SHEEP AND LAMB RHYMES

Little Bo Peep
Little Boy Blue
Baa Baa Black Sheep
Mary Had a Little Lamb

Little Bo Peep has lost her sheep
And doesn't know where to find them.
Leave them alone
And they'll come home,
Wagging their tails behind them.

 A traditional tune for this nursery rhyme can be found in Pamela Beall and Susan Nipp's *Wee Sing Nursery Rhymes and Lullabies* (Price, Stern & Sloan, 1985). *The Wee Sing* set comes with an audio cassette and sing-along book. It is easily found in most toy, book, or school-supply stores or can be ordered directly from Price, Stern & Sloan Publishers, Inc., 410 North La Cienega Boulevard, Los Angeles, CA 90048, 1-800-631-8571. This particular version includes two additional verses to sing.

Sing the song very, very slowly—in slow motion. Then sing the song very fast. Sing the song in a very high voice and then in a low, low voice. Challenge children to think of other ways to sing the song!

Encourage children to act out this nursery rhyme. Choose one child to be Little Bo Peep—the others are the sheep. The sheep wander around the area on all fours, then hide as you say the first two lines. Little Bo Peep shields her eyes with her hand and looks around for the sheep. She should look very sad when they are missing and very excited when they are found. On the last lines, the sheep hurry back to Little Bo Peep, wagging their bottoms on the last line. Children will want to act this out every time you say the rhyme!

Give each child an opportunity to play the part of Little Bo Peep. Use the child's name as you act out the rhyme—"Little *Courtney* Peep has lost her sheep. . . ."

Have each child illustrate an adaptation of the first line of the rhyme. Encourage children to complete the sentence using pets or animals [(Little (child's name) Peep has lost his or her (animal)] and then illustrate their lines with markers or crayons. More mature illustrators may want to draw the animal hiding behind something or Little Bo Peep crying. Use the pictures on a bulletin board with the title, "You Can't Pull the Wool Over My Eyes!" When you have enjoyed the pictures, take them down and bind them together for a class book. Make a cover for the book by inviting a child to illustrate Little Bo Peep and her sheep or by photocopying the illustration on page 33.

Write the rhyme on chart paper using picture symbols for the words *Little Bo Peep, sheep, home,* and *tails.* (See pages 268–272 for pictures you can use.) Laminate the chart. Then write the words for the symbols on sticky notes and have children match the words to the symbols.

Using the laminated chart from the previous activity, call out letters or words for individuals to come up and circle with a wipe-off marker. For example, they could put a red cross on the first word of the poem, circle the word *sheep*, put a blue rectangle around all of the *a*'s, put an orange triangle around each period, circle each word with a short vowel sound, or underline rhyming words.

After you have tried the above activity for several days, give each child a copy of the rhyme and a set of crayons. Call out directions and have children follow the directions on their own copies. For example, "Put a red X on each comma in the rhyme, circle all the lowercase *e*'s with green, circle two rhyming words with purple, underline a word that rhymes with *Joe* with a blue crayon."

Circle the word *sheep* on the laminated chart. Help children brainstorm a list of words that have the *-eep* ending, such as *jeep*, *asleep*, *beep*, *peep*, *sleep*, *keep*, and *deep*. Add to the list for several days. Then help children make their own sentence-strip flip books. Write the ending *-eep* on sentence strips. Copy the beginning sounds of the rhyming words onto smaller strips of all one size. Staple these beginning letters, one on top of the other, onto the left side of the *-eep* sentence strips. Children turn the beginning letter(s) to make new words. Keep a list of other words that rhyme with *sheep*, but are spelled differently, such as *heap*. Discuss the differences.

Place a small doll or wooden-block girl and some plastic or rubber sheep from a toy farm set in the block center. Encourage children to act out the rhyme with the figures.

Cut from felt for your flannel board: 10 white sheep, a little girl, and a brown crook. Manipulate the pieces as you recite the verse below. Teach children to sing the following words about Bo Peep and her sheep to the tune of the "Angel Band" while using the felt pieces. Children can also practice the song using their hands, popping up one finger for each number.

There was 1, there were 2, there were 3 little she-ep

There were 4, there were 5, there were 6 little she-ep

There were 7, there were 8, there were 9 little she-ep

10 little she-ep lost their way.

(Clapping) Oh wasn't that a day the sheep were lost,

Sheep were lost, sheep were lost.

Wasn't that a day the sheep were lost,

'Til Bo Peep brought them home.

Children will especially enjoy Paul Galdone's *Little Bo Peep* (Clarion, 1986) once they are familiar with the original version. Galdone's expanded version has the pretty blue-eyed Bo Peep finding her sheep, but they have lost their tails. She finds the tails hanging in a tree and ties them back on with red bows!

Most versions of Little Bo Peep show Bo Peep with a crook or staff. Point out the crook (not the bad guy on TV!) in the pictures and explain to children that watching the sheep was Little Bo Peep's job and that the crook was her tool. She was a shepherdess. Encourage children to make crooks with play dough or clay. First form a thick snake or rope, then bend the top to form the crook. After children have mastered making play dough crooks, encourage them to roll and bake crooks from sugar-cookie dough or breadstick dough for snacks.

Children will enjoy *The Shepherd Boy* by Kim Lewis (Four Winds Press, 1990) a beautifully illustrated tale describing a real shepherd boy who waits patiently until he is old enough to get his very own sheepdog, a crook, and a whistle to call the sheep.

More mature students will enjoy making up number problems about Bo Peep and her sheep. For example, Bo Peep lost 6 sheep. She found 1. How many are still lost? Or, Bo Peep has 4 sheep, but 3 are lost. How many does she still have? Use cotton balls or white pompoms as counters if needed.

Put out markers and crayons and have children practice using shapes to draw Bo Peep and her sheep. Show them how to make Bo Peep using a circle head, a triangle body, and stick arms and legs. Her staff is a lowercase *f* without the crossbar. Make the sheep using a cloud-shaped body, a smaller cloud-shaped head, four legs, and a wavy little tail. Once children see how easily shapes can be used to create pictures, they will enjoy illustrating this rhyme and the number problems they make up. Encourage more mature children to add details to complete their pictures.

Play the game Little Bo Peep has lost her sheep using the same rules as hide and seek (indoors) or chase (outdoors). "Bo Peep" hides her eyes and counts to 10 or 20 before beginning to look for the "sheep." Change the name of the game to the name of the child playing Bo Peep (Little Gabrielle Peep has lost her sheep). When Bo Peep finds the first sheep, that child becomes Bo Peep.

Read Matt Novak's *While the Shepherd Slept* (Orchard Books, 1991) in which a shepherd falls asleep and his sheep go to the theater to perform. After their performance they return to the meadow where the shepherd compliments them after awakening. He thinks they are such good sheep because they never wander! After reading this book, ask the children if they think that Bo Peep's sheep were at the theater when they were "lost." Brainstorm a list of other things the sheep might have been doing. Encourage children to write stories about the sheeps' adventures.

Laminate some white sheep shapes. Have one child be Bo Peep and hide all the sheep around the room while the others close their eyes and count. When all the sheep have been hidden, children search for them. The child who finds the most sheep gets to hand out treats to the class (a raisin or mini-marshmallow).

Play pin the tail on Bo Peep's sheep just as you would play pin the tail on the donkey. Enlarge a sheep pattern on white tagboard and laminate for durability. Give each child a large pompom or cotton ball, blindfold them one at a time, and have them place their tails on the sheep. Make a mark where the tails land. The child with the tail closest to where it should be gets to pass out a treat to the class.

Read the delightful *Each Peach Pear Plum* by Janet and Allan Ahlberg (Puffin Books, 1986). Children find a nursery or fairy-tale character, including Bo Peep, on each page. This is a good book to share with a single child in your lap or to suggest that parents read to their children at home.

Little Boy Blue, come blow your horn.
The sheep's in the meadow, the cow's in the corn.
Where's the little boy who looks after the sheep?
He's under the haystack fast asleep.

To introduce this rhyme, enlarge the illustration above, color, and mount on a large piece of tagboard. Ask children to predict what they think the rhyme is about. With the class, label the vocabulary in the picture (*Little Boy Blue, horn, sheep, meadow, cow, corn, haystack*). Children may find other things to label that do not directly relate to the poem, which is fine. Go over these words each day, underlining those that specifically relate to the rhyme. Encourage children to use magnetic or laminated letters to spell the underlined words.

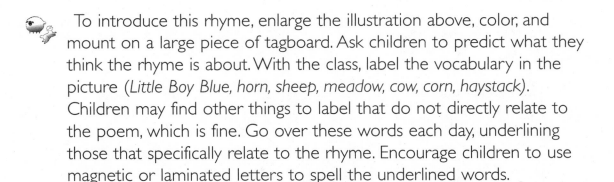

Match words to pictures in a pocket chart. Write the main nouns from the poem on sentence strips (*Little Boy Blue*, *horn*, *sheep*, *cow*, *corn*, *haystack*) and cut the strips in half. On the blank halves, illustrate the nouns with simple drawings, ask children to illustrate them, or use the illustrations on pages 268–272. Encourage children to match the words with the pictures in the pockets. You can use the word cards or illustrations as flashcards or to hold up as children recite the verse.

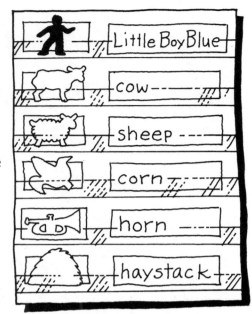

 A traditional tune for this nursery rhyme can be found in Pamela Beall and Susan Nipp's *Wee Sing Nursery Rhymes and Lullabies* (Price, Stern & Sloan, 1985). The *Wee Sing* set comes with an audio cassette and sing-along book. It is easily found in most toy, book, or school-supply stores or can be ordered directly from Price, Stern & Sloan Publishers, Inc., 410 North La Cienega Boulevard, Los Angeles, CA 90048.

Teach the class the nursery rhyme with the following motions.

Little Boy Blue come blow your horn.	Pretend to blow horn.
The sheep's in the meadow,	Look left and b-a-a like a sheep.
The cow's in the corn.	Look right and m-o-o like a cow.
Where's the little boy who looks after the sheep?	Palms up beside shoulders, questioning
He's under the haystack, fast asleep.	Whisper sh-h-h or hide under yellow blanket. Pretend to sleep

Show children a picture of the rhyme and ask them to suggest reasons why the sheep's in the meadow and the cow's in the corn!

 Have children make horns from cardboard tissue tubes. Spray-paint or use acrylic paint to color each horn. Encourage children to add decorations with permanent markers. Cut pieces of wax paper to fit over one end of each tube and hold in place with rubber bands. For younger children, use hot glue around the tube before putting on the rubber band (or you will spend your time putting the wax paper and rubber band on again and again as children investigate how it comes off!) Children blow in the open end, using the horn like a kazoo (or you may simply use kazoos or birthday horns).

 Have children hide their horns behind their backs and say the rhyme. At the end of the first line, children take their horns from behind their backs and blow, blow, blow. Then on your signal, they stop, put the horns behind their backs, and finish the poem. Children will love blowing their horns, so use that enthusiasm and have them march around the room, walk backwards around the room, in slow motion, and so on as you play a tape of nursery rhyme songs. They walk, dance, blow to the music but *stop* when the music stops!

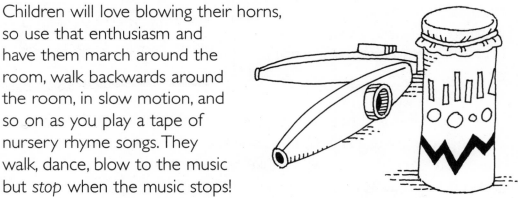

Discuss with children the fact that Little Boy Blue and Little Bo Peep had similar jobs. They looked after the sheep. They were shepherds, a word that comes from the words *sheep* and *herd*. Discuss how they handled their jobs differently. Ask children why Little Boy Blue might have fallen asleep on the job.

 Invite children to substitute their names and make pictures to illustrate the first line of the verse. For example, "Little Kelsey Blue, come blow your horn." Children might use blue markers or crayons to draw pictures of themselves all dressed in blue and blowing horns. Ellison-die horn cutouts work well for this project. Under each picture, write the appropriate line (*Little Kelsey Blue . . .*). Hang the pictures on the bulletin board for children to enjoy and then bind the pictures into a class book. Make a cover by inviting a child to illustrate Little Boy Blue with his horn, or photocopy the illustration on page 39.

Some children still need work identifying colors and color words. Take the opportunity to reinforce this skill with "Little Boy Blue." Children may make their own books to take home. Prepare photocopied or computer-generated pages of the words below—a page for each basic color. Have children illustrate each page, using markers or crayons of the appropriate color.

Little Boy Purple has no horn.

Little Boy Red has no horn.

Little Boy Orange has no horn . . .

Little Boy Blue, come blow your horn.

The sheep's in the meadow,

The cow's in the corn . . .

Make a game of identifying colors and color words. Draw or photocopy and color a boy for each of the colors (a blue boy, a red boy, a green boy, and so on). Cut out horn shapes from tagboard and write one of the color words on each horn. Children match each "boy" to his color-word horn.

Bring in fresh sweet corn for children to shuck. Consider shucking the corn into a dry water table, a dish pan, or outside. Help children identify the husk, kernels, cob, and silks. Pull off the husks and silks and clean the corn with a vegetable brush. Break the ears in two and cook in boiling water. Cool and serve at snacktime.

Help children make a list of things that are made from corn, such as cornbread, popcorn, and creamed corn. Make cornbread or popcorn for a snack.

Fill your sand table with cornmeal, unpopped corn kernels, or popcorn. If children each bring in some of the desired item, the table will fill quickly. Add some measuring and pouring items. Ask children which line of the rhyme you are identifying.

Make a mural to illustrate this rhyme. Have children add torn scraps of green paper to a large sheet of bulletin-board paper for the meadow (you can add a little real grass as well). Sheep can be precut or drawn on white paper and cut out. Add a little cotton to each sheep and place in the meadow. Then add long strips of green paper for rows of corn. Precut some corn shapes and have children glue popcorn kernels or corn husk pieces to the yellow corn and place in the cornfield. Make a fence around the cornfield area from wooden craft sticks. Have children draw and cut out black and brown cows or add precut cow shapes to the cornfield. Make a haystack out of brown or yellow construction paper and attach some real hay or pieces of shredded wheat. Have one child draw Little Boy Blue on a large sheet of drawing paper. Cut out, add a horn, and attach to the mural.

Make haystacks for snacktime.

Haystacks

1 Tb peanut butter

3-oz can chow mein noodles

1 c dried peanuts

6-oz pkg butterscotch morsels

Melt peanut butter and butterscotch morsels over low heat. Add noodles and peanuts and stir until well coated. Form clusters on foil and refrigerate. Makes about 2 dozen.

Fill a dishpan or dry water table with hay. Include some pieces of string and yarn and encourage children to bundle the hay into haystacks. Add some wooden or plastic toy people who can hide under the haystacks.

Add hay cut into 2-inch lengths to yellow play dough in the play dough area. Encourage children to form haystack shapes with the yellow play dough and then stick on the hay pieces to make haystacks. Add a small bowl of unpopped popcorn and have children form thick play dough snakes for corncobs and press the kernels into the "cobs." Add some small plastic farm animals (cows and sheep) and a small toy person that can be used as a farmer. Encourage children to act out the rhyme at the play dough table.

Baa baa black sheep,
Have you any wool?
Yes sir, yes sir, three bags full.
One for my master and one for the dame,
And one for the little boy that lives down the lane.

To introduce this rhyme, enlarge the above illustration on a photocopier, color, and mount on tagboard. Have children predict what they think the rhyme is about. With the class, label the vocabulary in the picture (*black sheep*, *three bags*, *little boy*, *lane*). Children may find other things to label that do not directly relate to the poem, which is fine. Go over the identified words each day, underlining those that specifically relate to the rhyme.

Encourage children to use magnetic or precut letters to spell the underlined words from the activity above, or make matching word and picture cards to go in a pocket chart.

Write the main nouns from the rhyme (*black sheep, three bags, master, dame, little boy*) on short sentence strips. Have volunteers illustrate each word on an index card or use the drawings on pages 268–272. Leave the words and pictures in a pocket chart so that children can match the words with the appropriate illustrations.

A traditional tune for this nursery rhyme can be found in Pamela Beall and Susan Nipp's *Wee Sing Nursery Rhymes and Lullabies* (Price, Stern & Sloan, 1985). The *Wee Sing* set comes with an audio cassette and sing-along book. It is easily found in most toy, book, or school-supply stores or can be ordered directly from Price, Stern & Sloan Publishers, Inc., 410 North La Cienega Boulevard, Los Angeles, CA 90048, 1-800-631-8571.

Read Moira Kemp's board book *Baa Baa Black Sheep* (Lodestar, 1991) with its adorable illustrations and line-by-line verse. Another good book for young children due to its larger size is *Start With Rhymes: Baa Baa Black Sheep* by Aidan Warlow (Wright Group, 1988).

Write the rhyme on chart paper using picture symbols for *sheep, bag, master, dame,* and *little boy*. Laminate for durability. Write the words for each picture on small sticky notes. Encourage children to place the sticky notes over the appropriate picture symbols on the laminated chart.

Each day after reading the poem, have children come up and circle words, letters, or language conventions in the rhyme, such as proper names, rhyming words, capital letters, words with the long e, or words with a silent e at the end, using washable markers.

 Write the entire rhyme on four sentence strips—one line per strip. Have children use these strips to match lines of the poem. Encourage individuals or small groups to use the laminated chart as a guide to putting the sentence strips in order.

Invite children to watch you cut the sentence strips from the above activity into individual words. Place these individual words in order in a pocket chart. Read the rhyme together with the class. Then have the children close their eyes while one child comes up and turns a word backwards. Children open their eyes and guess the mystery word. The child who guesses the word correctly takes the next turn.

 After you have cut the rhyme into individual words, distribute the word cards to children. Using the rhyme on the chart as a guide, have children form each line of the verse by bringing the words for that line to the front and holding the words in front of them. Help children line up in the same order as the sentence words or have children place the words in order into the pocket chart. Read the line as a class while children are standing and then go to the next line.

 After the words are cut apart, help children put them in alphabetical order. Or use the individual words to make an alphabet graph by writing the letters of the alphabet across the bottom of the chalkboard. Put a piece of double-sided tape on the back of each word and place each one above its initial letter. Discuss the graph. How many words begin with b? Which letter has the most words? Which letters have no words?

Use the words as sight-word flashcards or challenge groups or individual children to put the rhyme back together with or without the laminated chart as a guide.

After children have memorized the original verse, read Marilyn Janovitz's *Baa Baa Black Sheep* (Hyperion Books, 1991), which illustrates the rhyme line-by-line but which veers from the original words. Then try saying or singing the verse, substituting children's names and asking each if they have any wool. Each child answers with the names of three friends.

> You ask:
>
> *Trevor, Trevor,* have you any wool?
>
> Trevor answers:
>
> Yes sir, yes sir, three bags full.
>
> One for *Amanda,* one for *Johnny*
>
> and one for *Kelly* and that is all!

After you have gone around the circle and given each child a chance to answer, give children drawing paper with the poem innovation written at the bottom with blanks for their friends' names. Each child fills in the blanks with names of his or her choice. Have children use markers or crayons to illustrate the rhyme with three friends and three bags of wool.

 After studying "Little Bo Peep," "Little Boy Blue," and "Baa Baa Black Sheep," make a list of *b* words with the class. Leave the list up and add to it as the weeks go by.

For children who need to work on identifying colors or color words, make a big book using colors as follows.

> **Baa baa red sheep, have you any wool?**
>
> *No sir, no sir.*
>
> **Baa baa orange sheep, have you any wool?**
>
> *No sir, no sir.*
>
> **Baa baa yellow sheep, have you any wool?**
>
> *No sir, no sir . . . and so on.*

Baa baa black sheep, have you any wool?

Yes sir, yes sir, three bags full.

One for my master, one for the dame

And one for the little boy who lives down the lane!

On each page, write the words and place a construction-paper sheep cut from the appropriate color or a sheep outline for children to color. On the last page, add a black sheep and have children illustrate the master, the dame, and the little boy. You'll be amazed how fast children will learn to "read" this new book. You might also have children make their own little books to take home and read by photocopying the words and having children attach colored-paper sheep to the appropriate pages.

 Look at the language chunk *Baa baa black sheep, have you any wool?* and have children change the words for other animals.

Moo, moo, brown cow, have you any milk?

Quack, quack, yellow duck, have you any eggs?

Oink, oink, pink pig, have you any bacon?

Write each new choice on a sentence strip and place in a pocket chart. If children have difficulty reading the new lines, have volunteers illustrate each line on an index card. Glue these illustrations to the ends of the sentence strips.

Children will enjoy Ragnhild Scamell's *Three Bags Full* (Orchard Books, 1993). This story is not based on the nursery rhyme but is the story of Millie the lamb who gives up her fleece to her friends when they ask, and then gets very cold when snow comes. The farmer's wife has to knit her a sweater to keep her warm. It teaches children that lambs grow wool to keep warm in the winter and the fleece is sheared in the heat of the summer. See if children can guess where the author got his idea for the title of the book.

 Read *Black Sheep* by Elizabeth Heck (Little Brown, 1985) which is not based on the nursery rhyme but is simply about a black sheep with a mind of its own. Ask children what they think it means when someone says "he is the black sheep of the family" (different from the rest of the family, with a mind of his own).

Mary had a little lamb,
Its fleece was white as snow.
And everywhere that Mary went
The lamb was sure to go.

It followed her to school one day,
Which was against the rule.
It made the children laugh and play
To see a lamb at school.

A traditional tune for this nursery rhyme can be found in Pamela Beall and Susan Nipp's *Wee Sing Nursery Rhymes and Lullabies* (Price, Stern & Sloan, 1985). The *Wee Sing* set comes with an audio cassette and sing-along book. It is easily found in most toy, book, or school-supply stores or can be ordered directly from Price, Stern & Sloan Publishers, Inc., 410 North La Cienega Boulevard, Los Angeles, CA 90048.

After learning the original rhyme, take turns singing the names of children in the class in place of *Mary*.

"Mary Had a Little Lamb" was originally written by Sarah Josepha Hale in 1830. Each of the following three books gives a brief history of the poem and information about Sarah Hale, with its own artistic interpretation.

Hale, Sarah. *Mary Had a Little Lamb*. Holiday House, 1984 (illustrated by Tomie dePaola).

Hale, Sarah. *Mary Had a Little Lamb*. Orchard Books, 1995 (illustrated with fabric relief by Salley Mavor).

Hale, Sarah. *Mary Had a Little Lamb*. Scholastic, 1990 (illustrated with color photographs).

Have children make pictures of the poem on sheets of blue construction paper. Tear sheets of green construction paper in half and glue the half-sheets to the bottoms of the blue sheets to represent grass. Have each child draw Mary on white paper and cut around her.

For lambs, use sheets from small die-cut sheep note pads, have children trace and cut out sheep stencils, or have them draw sheep freehand. Children can add a little cotton to the sheep. They can draw schoolhouses, use sheets of die-cut schoolhouse note pads, or trace around schoolhouse stencils. Encourage children to use scraps of paper to add other details.

Invite children to act out the rhyme. Choose one child to be Mary and one to be the lamb. Make sure the lamb can "b-a-a-a"! Invite children to arrange a schoolhouse area with some desks and books. Choose a few children to be the children at school and one to be the teacher. As the class recites the rhyme, the actors play their parts: Mary walks to school, the lamb (on all fours, of course, and with a few b-a-a-as) follows obediently, the children "laugh and play" (point and giggle), and the teacher frowns and sends the lamb away. Continue until all children have had a chance to play a part.

Read Tomie dePaola's interpretation of "Mary Had a Little Lamb," which shows children in class with their pets. Identify each pet and then invite children to tell about their own pets. Adapt the language chunk (*Child's name*) *had a little* (*pet*) and have children complete the sentence to describe themselves. Write or have the child write the line at the bottom of a piece of paper and illustrate it with a picture of him- or herself and the pet. Children without a pet can draw themselves with a pet they would like to have. Put the pictures on a bulletin board with the title "<u>Mary</u> Had a Little <u>Lamb</u>!" When children have enjoyed the pictures for a while, take them down and bind them into a class book. You will be surprised at how quickly children are able to "read" this book. Children will also enjoy singing their verses to the "Mary Had a Little Lamb" tune.

Look for the wonderful rebus rhyme of "Mary Had a Little Lamb" in Tedd Arnold's *Mother Goose's Words of Wit and Wisdom* (Dial Books for Young Readers, 1990). This is a beautiful collection of nursery rhymes illustrated with cross-stitch and other needlework. Children will especially enjoy being able to "read" this illustrated rebus version of "Mary Had a Little Lamb."

Brainstorm with children all the possible words that might fill in the blank: "Mary had a _____ lamb." For example, *fat, thin, big, little, humongous, black, blue, sad*. Have volunteers illustrate Mary with each lamb. Write the appropriate sentence at the bottom of each illustration and bind into a class book.

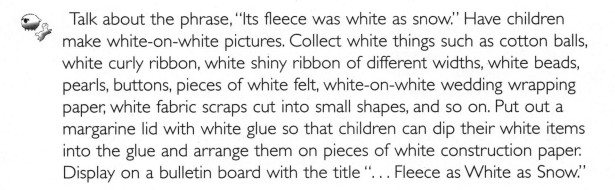

Talk about the phrase, "Its fleece was white as snow." Have children make white-on-white pictures. Collect white things such as cotton balls, white curly ribbon, white shiny ribbon of different widths, white beads, pearls, buttons, pieces of white felt, white-on-white wedding wrapping paper, white fabric scraps cut into small shapes, and so on. Put out a margarine lid with white glue so that children can dip their white items into the glue and arrange them on pieces of white construction paper. Display on a bulletin board with the title ". . . Fleece as White as Snow."

Have children brainstorm other colors and words that might fit in the blanks ". . . its fleece was_____ as _____" For example, its fleece was green as grass, its fleece was black as coal, its fleece was blue as the sky, its fleece was red as a fire engine.

Look for schoolhouse note pads, small and large, and sheep note pads, small and large, to make flashcards (available from Carson-Dellosa or Shapes, Etc.). Flashcard skills might include numeral recognition, number word recognition, color word recognition, spelling and sight words, or whatever is appropriate for your group. Or use large schoolhouse note pads and small lamb note pads for matching skills (numerals to number words, letters to initial or final consonant sounds, vowels to pictures depicting their sounds, and so on).

Sheep and Lamb Activities

Magnetic Way (Creative Edge, Inc.) makes a series of pictures that cling to a special board. One of the picture series available is nursery rhymes. All four of these sheep and lamb rhymes are included. The pieces can be used to illustrate the rhymes and can then be left out for children to manipulate, much like a flannel board.

Make an audio tape to go with this unit. Include some songs recorded commercially as well as individual students and the class reciting and singing each of the rhymes.

Children will enjoy this activity after they have memorized several nursery rhymes. Select any collection of nursery rhymes and show children each page, asking "Do we know this rhyme?" This helps teach children the importance of using picture clues to identifying text. If they say no, turn pages until children find a rhyme they recognize. Ask children which pictures gave them clues and then recite the rhyme with children. Continue all the way through the book. Select a different collection of rhymes each day.

Ask children where they think they might find information about sheep. Take them to the library and help them select some appropriate books. Here are some sheep facts that you might want to teach.

The father sheep is a ram, and the mother sheep is a ewe.

Baby sheep are lambs.

Sheep usually have one or two baby lambs, called twins, at a time.

Occasionally they have triplets.

Baby lambs drink milk from their moms.

Sheep have long hair, which is called fleece.

When the fleece gets long, it is sheared and used to make woolen thread and yarn that is made into cloth.

Sheep are grown for their wool and meat. Other by-products are soap, glue, and cosmetics.

The person who tends the sheep is called a shepherd or a shepherdess and usually carries a crook or staff. He or she often has a sheep dog to help.

A wonderful book about the first two weeks of a lamb's life is the black-and-white photojournal *Lambing Time* by Jane Miller (Routledge, 1978).

The processes of shearing and weaving cloth are described in Tomie dePaola's *Charlie Needs a Cloak* (Simon & Schuster, 1982), Elsa Beskow's *Pelle's New Suit* (Harper, 1961), and *A New Coat for Anna* by Harriet Ziefert and Anita Lobel (Knopf Books for Young Readers, 1988), which is best for more mature listeners.

The beautifully illustrated *The Shepherd Boy* by Kim Lewis (Four Winds Press, 1990) describes a child's wait to become a real shepherd with a crook, sheep dog, and whistle.

Draw a sheep on a piece of white tagboard, photocopy the picture on page 271, or use a sheet from a sheep note pad. Put the picture at the top of the tagboard and write the word *sheep*. Use information gleaned from books about sheep to help the children make a chart of basic information.

look	fleece
say	B-a-a!
live	farms/pastures
eat	hay and grass
give	wool, meat, soap, glue, cosmetics
have	baby lambs

Sheep Facts

look
fleece

say
"Baa!"

live
farms
pastures

eat
grass
hay

give
wool

have
baby
lambs

Use the information to chant with the class. Clap hands to a steady beat. Lead the chant yourself, but stop before the underlined words so that children may say them.

This is how the sheep look, sheep look, sheep look,

This is how the sheep look. Sheep have fleece.

This is what the sheep say, sheep say, sheep say,

This is what the sheep say. Sheep say "B-a-a!"

Bring in some real lambswool and articles made from wool. Let children feel each item and explain that they are all made of wool from a lamb or sheep. Children will often ask if it hurts the sheep when the fleece is sheared. Explain that it is much like getting a haircut or cutting your fingernails—doesn't hurt a bit and grows right back.

Explain to children that fleece that is sheared from sheep is turned into yarn. Use yarn for this art project. Clip 12-inch (30 cm) strands of yarn to clothespins. Put three colors of paint into three plastic foam meat trays. Holding the clothespin, dip a strand into each tray of paint. Use a popsicle stick or plastic knife to help coat the yarn with paint. When it is coated, lift it out and drag it across a piece of construction paper to make an abstract painting.

  Make colorful yarn weavings on plastic foam meat trays. Make half-inch slits an inch apart along the top and bottom of each tray. Use the slits to anchor a strand of yarn as you wrap it evenly around the tray four or five times, taping the ends underneath. Attach a piece of yarn to a popsicle-stick-needle and have children weave the string back and forth in an over-and-under fashion until they have used the entire strand of yarn. Tie on a new color and continue. Hang these colorful projects on a bulletin board with the title "Can't Pull the Wool Over My Eyes!"

  Write numbers down the left side of a sheet of paper. Children may glue the appropriate number of cotton balls or stamp the appropriate number of sheep, using a sheep rubber stamp from a farm animal rubber stamp set beside each number.

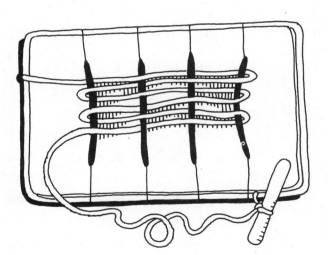

Make a manipulative number game using sheep note pads. Glue each sheep to a piece of tagboard and write a number on each sheep. Laminate for durability. Using black and white pompoms as counters, children count the appropriate number of pompoms onto each sheep. More mature students can make addition problems for each sheep by adding a number of white pompoms and a number of black pompoms to make the numbers on the sheep cards.

Look for large sheep-shaped note pads that children can glue to a piece of construction paper. Give children cotton balls to glue onto the sheep for a nice soft lamb.

Use sheep note pads to make flashcards using numerals, letters, color words, sight words, or name recognition. Look for the large and small sheep note pads from Shapes, Etc. to use for matching skills (match the baby lamb to the larger mother). Consider skills such as matching uppercase to lowercase letters, matching initial or final letters to appropriate pictures, vowels to pictures of vowel sounds, numerals to number words.

Glue a large sheep note pad sheet to tagboard and trim the tagboard around the shape. Laminate for durability and punch holes around the perimeter. Add a strand of yarn (dip one end in white glue and let dry) and use the sheep for a lacing card. Children can make their own lacing cards to take home or you can make one for the manipulative center.

Encourage children to make sheep from white play dough. Sheep cookie cutters can be found with farm cookie-cutter sets in the spring.

Tape episodes of *Lambchop* for children to watch (explain to children that Lambchop is a lamb). Look for books, puppets, and videos featuring Lambchop that children might enjoy.

Plan a field trip to a farm that has sheep and lambs. Try to go at a time when you can see newborn lambs or the shearing of the sheep. Ask to bring back some of the fleece for art projects. Have a parent videotape the field trip for a culmination activity when you get back to school.

At your book center, have an assortment of books that feature sheep and lambs as the main characters to give children ideas for their own stories and artwork. Read some to the class each day, making sure to teach and discuss as you go. The following are only a few of the possibilities.

Alda, Arlene. *Sheep, Sheep, Sheep Help Me Fall Asleep*. Doubleday, 1992.

Archambault, John. *Counting Sheep*. Henry Holt & Company, 1989.

Blanchard, Arlene. *The Naughty Lamb*. Dial Books, 1989.

Brenner, Barbara. *Lion and Lamb Step Out*. Bantam, 1990.

Bursik, Rose. *Zoe's Sheep*. Henry Holt and Company, 1994.

DePaola, Tomie. *Haircuts for the Woolseys*. Putnam, 1989.

Enderle, Judith R. and Stephanie G. Tressler. *Six Creepy Sheep*. Boyds Mills Press, 1992.

Enderle, Judith R. and Stephanie G. Tressler. *Six Snowy Sheep*. Boyds Mills Press, 1994.

Ernst, Lisa C. *Nattie Parson's Good-Luck Lamb*. Puffin Books, 1990.

Gordon, Jeffie Ross. *Six Sleepy Sheep*. Caroline House, 1991.

Ichikawa, Satomi. *Nora's Surprise*. Putnam, 1994.

Kitamura, Satoshi. *When Sheep Cannot Sleep: A Counting Book*. Farrar Straus and Giroux, 1988.

Lewis, Kim. *Emma's Lamb*. Macmillan Children's Books, 1991.

O'Brien, Mary. *Counting Sheep to Sleep*. Little, Brown, 1992.

Shaw, Nancy. *Sheep in a Jeep*. Houghton Mifflin, 1986.

Shaw, Nancy. *Sheep in a Shop*. Houghton Mifflin, 1992.

Shaw, Nancy. *Sheep on a Ship*. Houghton Mifflin, 1992.

Shaw, Nancy. *Sheep Out to Eat*. Houghton Mifflin, 1992.

Wellington, Monica. *The Sheep Follow*. Dutton's Children's Books, 1992.

KING AND QUEEN RHYMES

Humpty Dumpty

Old King Cole

Queen of Hearts

Sing a Song of Sixpence

Humpty Dumpty sat on a wall.
Humpty Dumpty had a great fall.
All the king's horses and all the king's men
Couldn't put Humpty together again.

Photocopy, enlarge if you wish, and color the above illustration. Mount it on tagboard. Have children discuss the picture and predict what they think might happen or what has already happened. With the class, label the vocabulary in the picture by drawing lines out from each identified item and writing the words: *Humpty Dumpty, wall, king's horses,* and *king's men.* Children will find other things in the picture to label that do not relate directly to the poem, which is fine.

Each day, go over the words that the class has identified on the picture, underlining those that specifically relate to the rhyme. Encourage children to use magnetic or precut letters to spell the underlined words. Encourage children to write and illustrate each word as well.

A traditional tune for this nursery rhyme can be found in Pamela Beall and Susan Nipp's *Wee Sing Nursery Rhymes and Lullabies* (Price, Stern & Sloan, 1985). The *Wee Sing* set comes with an audio cassette and sing-along book. It is easily found in most toy, book, or school-supply stores or can be ordered directly from Price, Stern & Sloan Publishers, Inc., 410 North La Cienega Boulevard, Los Angeles, CA 90048.

Give each child a turn to sit on a "wall" and then "fall" at the appropriate moment. Children can recite just the first two lines or create an innovation using each child's name.

Christina Dumpty sat on a wall.

Christina Dumpty had a great fall.

Even Mrs. Timmons and all the class children

Could not put Christina together again.

or

Christina Dumpty sat on a wall.

Christina Dumpty had a great fall.

And then Mrs. Timmons and all the class children

Helped put Christina together again!

Humpty Dumpty is an all-time favorite, so be ready for children to thoroughly enjoy themselves acting out this rhyme again and again. Have the class recite the rhyme while a few children play the parts of Humpty and the king's men. Turn a rocking boat (or crate) on its side for Humpty's wall. Make a few crowns for the king's men and add robes, if you like, made from pieces of fabric clothespinned at the neck Batman-style. The king's men can gallop around on stick horses and then stop and help put Humpty together again by helping him back onto the wall. Or they can simply pass by, shaking their heads as if there's nothing to be done. Purchase stick horses or make your own by cutting two horse-head patterns from tagboard. Decorate with ribbon and markers. Glue or staple the horse-head sections together with a dowel or heavy cardboard tube (an empty wrapping-paper roll or tube from a roll of laminating film) in between. "Giddy-up!"

Alter the language chunk *Humpty Dumpty sat on a wall* to put each child in his or her own picture (*Sarah Dumpty sat on a wall*). Children illustrate themselves on the wall made of gray, brown, tan, or black construction paper "rocks" that you have torn or cut. Draw a line across the middle of a piece of blue construction paper and have children fill the bottom half with "rocks" to create a stone wall.

Children then draw themselves as Humpty Dumpty on white paper, cut around the self-portraits, and glue them atop the walls. Add the appropriate words to each child's picture and display on a bulletin board with the title "Join Humpty Dumpty on the Wall!" After children have enjoyed the pictures, take them down and bind them into a class book with a picture of Humpty on the wall for a cover.

Sarah Dumpty sat on a wall.

For artistic renderings of Humpty, begin with the brick wall. Give each child 1-inch wide strips of red construction paper to snip into "bricks." Children glue their bricks in lines across sheets of white construction paper. Then they glue their brick walls to the bottoms of large pieces of blue construction paper. Use stencils or precut white ovals for Humpty. Children can add features such as eyes (precut or gummed circles), bow ties, hats, wallpaper vests with real buttons, and accordion-pleated arms and legs. Put out scraps of construction paper to encourage children's creativity. Each Humpty should have his own distinct characteristics. Display with the title "Humpty Dumpty Sat on a Wall."

Encourage shape-drawing practice with this rhyme. Put out plenty of drawing paper, markers, crayons, and colored pencils. Show children how to draw Humpty Dumpty using shapes: an oval for his body, circles for his eyes, and so on. Encourage children to add other parts as their interests dictate—arms, legs, bow ties, hats, shoes, a wall, or whatever their imaginations come up with! To give reluctant artists a starting point, set out precut white ovals or oval stencils.

Help children enjoy putting Humpty Dumpty together again by making their own puzzles. Put out large oval stencils so children can trace and cut Humpty from white tagboard. Have children use markers or crayons to add features. Then cut each oval into pieces (as many as each child can handle—you can always cut each piece into more pieces as children become more competent). Put the puzzle pieces in envelopes for children to take home.

Humpty Dumpty is a perfect rhyme to sequence. Look for a nursery rhyme book that shows three or four pictures of Humpty, such as the illustration in James Marshall's nursery rhyme collection, *James Marshall's Mother Goose* (Farrar, Straus and Giroux, 1979). Photocopy the pictures (with permission), draw your own sequence with stick figures on unlined index cards, or have volunteers illustrate each line of the rhyme. Use the words *beginning*, *middle*, and *end* as you discuss the action. Leave the cards out for children to sequence independently. Copy (reduced, if necessary) the pictures onto a single sheet of white paper and photocopy. Have children cut out each picture, color, and then glue back in order on colorful strips of construction paper.

Create a class mural of Humpty Dumptys on a bulletin board. Start with a large red brick wall. Dip a rectangular chalkboard eraser into red paint to make brick prints along white bulletin-board paper for the wall—children will love doing this themselves! Give each child a large piece of white construction paper and have them cut ovals by rounding off the corners. Children fill the ovals with cut or torn white pieces of construction paper so that Humpty looks as if he's been put together again. They can add other features made from scrap paper as desired. Line the Humptys up on the "brick wall" with the title "Humpty Was a Very Good Egg!"

Have children brainstorm reasons why Humpty fell off the wall (he was pushed, he was dancing and missed a step, he was so fat that he just rolled off). Encourage creativity. Invite children to develop one of the ideas into their own stories, individually or in small groups.

Have children brainstorm ways that they could "fix" Humpty, such as by using Band-Aids, glue, tape, or staples. Then make a graph of the options. Write each child's name or glue a photograph of each child to a sticky note and have children indicate how they would fix Humpty by placing a sticky note on the graph. Discuss the choices and the completed graph. Then have children illustrate their chosen repair methods in art. Children cut large ovals from white construction paper, cut the eggs in two or more parts, and put them back together using Band-Aids, staples, tape, glue, or whatever they choose (be sure these items are available). Have children glue their put-back-together Humptys to colorful construction paper and display the pictures around the graph.

Collect a few white-plastic egg-shaped stocking containers to put in your sand table and some large red-plastic bricks to make a wall. Children will enjoy pretending that the eggs are Humpty (you can add features with a permanent marker or by hot-gluing felt pieces on) and having him break in two when he falls. Also put a couple of eggs at your building center, along with plastic blocks, wooden blocks, and wooden logs. The challenge for children is to build a wall and then have Humpty take a fall without breaking. Children will enjoy and expand on this play, often building Humpty a whole house with rooms for the family!

Have children enjoy the adventure of Humpty while making scrambled eggs—"Humpty's Eggs." You will need a raw egg for each child and a big sturdy bowl. Give each child a turn to sit his or her egg on the side of the bowl while the rest of the children recite the first two lines of the rhyme. Then each child makes the egg fall and break (they will find their own ways to do this!). Be prepared for a little eggshell in the eggs—that's why they are called Humpty's Eggs—and be prepared for at least one child to be concerned because they are going to eat Humpty! After all of the eggs are broken, have children take turns stirring. Add a little milk and pour into a frying pan sprayed with cooking oil or put in the microwave. Serve warm, not hot.

Reinforce cognitive skills with plastic eggs that come apart. To teach colors, collect colored plastic Easter eggs. Put the egg halves in your sand table and encourage children to match colored halves. Children will enjoy filling the eggs with sand and putting them back together. For other matching skills, collect plastic egg-shaped stocking containers or Easter eggs (using colored eggs may give children the additional clue of the color to use when matching, if necessary). Program different skills on opposite halves of the eggs with permanent marker. For example, write a numeral on one half and make that same number of dots on the other half. Or write an uppercase letter on one half and the lowercase letter on the other half.

Invite children to a Humpty Dumpty Egg Hunt. Put each child's name on a colored plastic egg (use washable marker so the eggs can be reused). Recite the rhyme with the class. When you get to the last word, children may hunt for their eggs. The only rule is that children are not allowed to find anyone else's eggs. You may wish to hide two or three for each child. When children have found their eggs, they sit quietly in a specified area. This is great name-recognition practice! Leave the eggs out so that children can organize their own games and hunts.

Collect plastic eggs in a basket to use as reinforcement in the way that a treasure box is used to reward good behavior. Put a small treat, such as a few M&Ms, a Hershey's kiss, or a balloon in each egg (check in dollar stores or in party favor departments). At the end of each day, invite children who have earned a treat to select an egg as their prize (they keep the treats and return the eggs). Bet you'll have the best-behaved Humpties in the school!

Boil an egg for each child (ask a parent to donate the eggs but if possible do the cooking in class). Cool the eggs and challenge each child to peel one—an experience in itself! Discuss how the rhyme would have changed if Humpty had been a hard-boiled egg! Invite children to taste the whites and then the yolks of their eggs. On the chalkboard, draw a large hard-boiled egg half (a yellow circle within a white oval). Children can place sticky notes with their names on them or small photos of themselves into the section they liked best. Discuss the results.

Save the eggshells in a colander in the sink, wash, and dry on paper towels for children to glue to white ovals (and put Humpty together again). Discuss with children why the king's men couldn't put Humpty back together. Could they put their eggs back together?

Put out white play dough and oval cookie cutters (available around Easter or with cookie-cutter shape sets) so children can make Humpty Dumpties. Encourage children to add facial features, arms, legs, and so on. Also add a few plastic foam egg cartons and suggest that children make a dozen eggs or a dozen "Humpty babies."

This is a good time to talk about other animals that come from eggs to help children understand the Humpty Dumpty riddle. Explain that Humpty was first an egg, then probably a chick, but that other animals lay eggs, too—ducks, geese, ostriches, and other birds; snakes; turtles; frogs; alligators; butterflies; fish; and dinosaurs. Children will enjoy the following books to reinforce this science concept.

Seven Eggs by Meredith Hooper. Harper and Row, 1985.

Chickens Aren't the Only Ones by Ruth Heller. Grosset and Dunlap, 1981.

An Extraordinary Egg by Leo Lionni. Alfred A. Knopf, 1994.

Good Morning, Chick by Mirra Ginsburg. Mulberry, 1989.

After children are familiar with this rhyme, they will enjoy Stephen Cosgrove's adaptation, *Favorite Fairy Tales: Humpity Dumpity*. In this rhyme the king and Humpity enjoy walking on the wall and playing together. But when Humpity falls, the king is upset until he realizes that Humpity is really a chick. Children will enjoy the delightful humor of this story.

 Have children write rhyming couplets based on other things Humpty Dumpty might have sat on.

Humpty Dumpty sat on a bird.
Humpty Dumpty was a nerd.

Humpty Dumpty sat on a table.
Humpty Dumpty was not stable.

Humpty Dumpty sat on a bat.
Humpty Dumpty should not have done that!

Encourage children to illustrate new couplets. Write the words under each illustration and display on a bulletin board.

Enjoy Colin and Jacqui Hawkins' *Humpty Dumpty* (Candlewick Press, 1992), a "fingerwiggle" board book with die-cut holes for children to put their fingers through. In the Humpty Dumpty rhyme, a child's fingers become Humpty's legs. If children enjoy this book, encourage them to make their own fingerwiggle Humptys by cutting oval Humptys from white tagboard (you will have to cut the finger holes). They can add clothes and facial features and then put their own two fingers through the holes to make Humpty walk.

Enjoy Sarah Hayes and Charlotte Voake's *Bad Egg: The True Story of Humpty Dumpty* (Joy Street Books, 1987) with the class. This book with predictable, rhyming text tells the story of the horses and king's men who join Humpty on the wall. After sharing this story, encourage children to use the same predictable text to write stories about others who might have joined Humpty on the wall—other nursery-rhyme characters, members of the class, farm animals, zoo animals, or family members.

Another favorite book based on the nursery rhyme is *Little Lumpty* by Miko Imai (Candlewick Press, 1994). Little Lumpty lives in the town of Dumpty and is very familiar with the story of Humpty, who lived long ago. However, Lumpty doesn't learn from the original story and insists on climbing to the top of that wall anyway. This time, however, the results are a little different. Children who love the adventure of Humpty Dumpty will certainly enjoy the antics of Lumpty!

Another fun book for children is Tom Ross' *Eggbert, the Slightly Cracked Egg* (Putnam, 1994). Eggbert, like Humpty, has his own adventures. After reading about Eggbert, encourage children to name an egg of their own—perhaps Egghead—and dictate or write their own adventure stories.

Also look for some of the rhymes in nursery-rhyme collections that put a positive twist to the end of this rhyme, such as Diane Loomans, Karen Kilberg, and Julia Loomans' *Positively Mother Goose* (Starseed Press, 1991). Children will probably prefer the original version, but they will enjoy hearing a different twist. Encourage them to write their own original endings to the verse.

Another adaptation of this rhyme is the 25-minute video *The Real Story of Humpty Dumpty* (Golden Book Video, 1990), a much-expanded version that includes the story of Humpty's birth, his early days on Mr. Dumpty's Farm, and adventures with Glitch the Witch and Princess Allegra.

Introduce Shel Silverstein's "Eggs Rated" from his poetry collection *Falling Up* (HarperCollins, 1996). The poem plays on many words that are spelled with *ex*, such as *eggceptional* and *eggspert*. Write the poem on chart paper and laminate. Have children come up and circle all the egg words with a washable marker. Discuss with children how the prefix *ex-* sounds like *eggs*. Make a list of *ex-* words that have the *eggs* sound and keep adding words as you or the children think of more.

Children will enjoy these other fiction and nonfiction books about eggs.

Fowler, Allan. *The Chicken or the Egg?* Childrens Press, 1993.

Hariton, Anca. *Egg Story*. Dutton, 1992.

Heine, Helme. *The Most Wonderful Egg in the World*. Margaret K. McElderry Books, 1983.

Jenkins, Priscilla. *Nest Full of Eggs*. HarperCollins, 1995.

Seuss, Dr. *Green Eggs and Ham*. Random House, 1960.

Seuss, Dr. *Horton Hatches the Egg*. Random House, 1968.

Old King Cole was a merry old soul
And a merry old soul was he.
He called for his pipe,
He called for his bowl,
And he called for his fiddlers three.

 Photocopy the above illustration, color if desired, and glue to a large piece of tagboard. Share the picture with children and have them predict what they think will happen in the rhyme. With the class, label the vocabulary in the picture: *Old King Cole, pipe, bowl, fiddlers*. Children will find other things in the picture to label that do not relate directly to the poem, which is fine. Go over the words that the class has identified each day, underlining those that relate specifically to the rhyme. Ask children what they think the word *merry* means (happy, cheerful). Ask them to show you *merry* (laughing, smiling). Also, as you identify fiddlers, ask children if they can remember another rhyme that contained a fiddle ("Hey diddle diddle, the cat and the fiddle . . ."). Ask children why they think the king would have called for his pipe, bowl, and fiddlers.

A traditional tune for this nursery rhyme can be found in Pamela Beall and Susan Nipp's *Wee Sing Nursery Rhymes and Lullabies* (Price, Stern & Sloan, 1985). The *Wee Sing* set comes with an audio cassette and sing-along book. It is easily found in most toy, book, or school-supply stores or can be ordered directly from Price, Stern & Sloan Publishers, Inc., 410 North La Cienega Boulevard, Los Angeles, CA 90048. This particular rhythmic version includes an innovation at the end of the rhyme.

Help children act out this rhyme by creating some props and costumes.

throne	chair (or something more elaborate)
king's crown	fast-food or construction-paper version
king's robe	piece of fabric tied or clothespinned at the neck, Batman-style
pipe	bubble pipe, real pipe, or black tagboard pipe
bowl	real bowl or tagboard bowl
three fiddles	brown tagboard violins and bows (dowels or sticks)

You will need one king, one child to bring the pipe, another to bring the bowl, and three children to "play" the fiddles. They can bring their assigned items and then bow to the king. Have the class recite the verse as children play their parts. The king might clap as he calls for each item.

Old King Cole was a merry old soul

And a merry old soul was he.

He called for his pipe, (clap, clap)

He called for his bowl, (clap, clap)

And he called for his fiddlers three. (clap, clap)

Write the rhyme on chart paper and laminate. Find pictures or use the ones on pages 268–272 for the words *pipe*, *bowl*, *fiddlers*, and *three*. Put double-sided tape or sticky-note glue on the backs of the pictures so children can match pictures to words on the chart.

Write the entire rhyme on sentence strips, one line per strip. Children can match the sentence strips to the lines of the rhyme on chart paper. Encourage both individuals and small groups of children to sequence the lines.

As children watch, cut the sentence strips from the above activity into individual words. Place the words in a pocket chart in order and read the rhyme with the class. Ask children to close their eyes and choose one child to come up and turn a word backwards. Children open their eyes and guess what the mystery word is. The child who guesses correctly takes the next turn.

After you have cut the rhyme into individual words, distribute the words to students. Display the rhyme on chart paper and challenge children to form each line of the rhyme by bringing the appropriate words, one at a time, to the front and placing them in order in the pocket chart. Read the completed line together and then go to the next line.

Put the cut-apart words in alphabetical order. Help children count the words in the rhyme (32).

Use the cut-apart words as sight-word flashcards or challenge groups or individual children to put the complete rhyme back together on the floor or in a pocket chart.

Introduce the words *soul, bowl,* and *Cole.* These are rhyming words with endings that sound alike but are not spelled alike. Make a list of other words that sound like these words, and discover others that are spelled differently (*knoll, roll, scroll, stroll, troll, toll*). Keep the list up for a week and add to it as chidren think of new words.

"He called for his pipe." Make bubble pipes from plastic foam cups for outside play. Poke holes for straws near the bottoms of the cups. Pour bubble solution into a flat plate. Dip the tops of the cups flat into the bubble solution, pick up the cup slowly, and blow! Wonderful bubbles!

Old King Cole lived before people knew that smoking is bad for your health. You can explain this rhyme by suggesting that the king called for his bubble pipe and then called for his bowl of bubble solution so he could blow bubbles while his fiddlers serenaded him. Or discuss with children some of the things that they would tell King Cole today about smoking a pipe and how it is bad for his health.

"He called for his bowl. . . ." Brainstorm with children a list of things that might have been in the king's bowl—porridge, bubble solution, goldfish, and so on. Have children illustrate at least one of the ideas, and write the words "He called for his bowl . . ." on the bottom of each illustration.

Review shapes by choosing a shape and color to represent each item in the nursery rhyme. For example,

large blue rectangle = king

small black square = pipe

small yellow circle = bowl

large purple ovals = fiddlers

small brown triangles = fiddles

Cut the shapes from felt so you can tell the story on your flannel board. After children are familiar with the rhyme, have them make individual shape books to take home and "read" to their families. Prepare pages with the words of the verse and have children add the appropriate shapes cut from colored construction paper. As you go through the story, review shapes and colors.

Page I
Old King Cole was a merry old soul
   And a merry old soul was he.   blue rectangle

Page 2
He called for his pipe,   blue rectangle + black
                                           square

Page 3
He called for his bowl,   blue rectangle + black
                                           square + yellow circle

Page 4

And he called for his fiddlers three.

blue rectangle + black square + yellow circle + 3 purple ovals with their 3 brown triangles

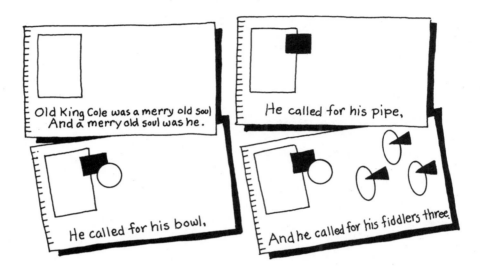

Old King Cole was a merry old soul
And a merry old soul was he.

He called for his pipe,

He called for his bowl,

And he called for his fiddlers three.

Or you can make individual flannel boards for children to use independently. Cover cigar boxes with self-adhesive plastic, hot-glue felt to the inside of the top, and cut small shapes (above) to illustrate the rhyme. Have children put the shapes on their miniature flannel boards as they recite the rhyme. Children can store the shapes inside the boxes.

Here's another version that children can take home to "read." Hold a large sheet of gray construction paper horizontally and fold the two ends into the center so the "castle" opens out from the middle. With the paper folded, cut rectangular chunks from across the top to create a crenellated castle.

Front cover, left side: *Old King Cole was a merry old soul* (write or have children write the verse throughout).

Front cover, right side: *And a merry old soul was he* (children draw pictures of King Cole).

Open, left side: *He called for his pipe* (children draw pipes or cut pipe shapes from black construction paper using stencils).

Open, right side: *He called for his bowl* (children draw bowls or cut bowls from colored construction paper using stencils).

Middle, inside: *And he called for his fiddlers three* (children draw three men with fiddles or cut three fiddle shapes from brown construction paper using stencils).

Enjoy *King Cole's Castle* by Colin and Moira Maclean (Kingfisher Books, 1992). This book involves King Cole in a lively new adventure in which the three fiddlers abandon him to play in a seaside band because they are tired of playing his favorite song. They eventually return after the king tries his hand at making music himself. Delightful!

More mature students will enjoy the Wee Sing video *King Cole's Party* (Price, Stern & Sloan, 1987) in which real people act out nursery rhymes in a story format. The main plot involves the people of the kingdom coming to King Cole's birthday party. Other nursery rhymes and nursery-rhyme characters make an appearance, including Humpty Dumpty. This video is an hour long, but is a delight to children who are familiar with the rhymes.

Explain to children that a fiddle is a violin. Invite someone to come in and play the violin for children—both classical and country "fiddle" music, if possible. Call your local symphony or high-school music director for suggestions. Perhaps your music teacher has a violin or recordings of violin music.

The Queen of Hearts,
She made some tarts,
All on a summer's day;
The Knave of Hearts,
He stole the tarts,
And with them ran away.
The King of Hearts
Called for the tarts,
And scolded the knave full score.
The Knave of Hearts
Brought back the tarts,
And vowed he'd steal no more!

Practice chanting this rhyme with children. Once chanting is mastered, use motions such as clapping, snapping fingers, and hitting thighs to keep a steady beat.

With the class, whisper the entire poem very softly, shout it out loud, say it very s-l-o-w-ly, and then say it really fast. After you have been through each version, give each child a turn and have the class guess if it was loud, soft, slow, fast, or something else. Children get lots of fun practice while memorizing the rhyme!

Write the rhyme on chart paper and laminate. Call out letters or words for individuals to circle with a wipe-off marker. For example, circle the word *queen*, put a red rectangle around all of the e's, put a green triangle around each period, or circle all the words with a short vowel sound. Discuss the word *knave* (a dishonest or deceitful person, a tricky rascal). It also refers to the Jack in a deck of playing cards (you may wish to substitute the word *jack* for *knave* throughout this study). Also discuss the silent *k* at the beginning of the word. See if children can think of other words that have the silent *k*.

After you have modeled circling words and letters and other language conventions on the laminated rhyme for a couple of days, give each child his or her own set of crayons and a paper copy of the rhyme. Call out some of the same directions so that children can mark their own copies.

This nursery rhyme sets the perfect stage for a values lesson. Talk with the children about stealing. What did the Knave of Hearts do? (He stole the tarts.) But what happened when he told the truth? (The king was mad, but the knave returned the tarts and said he wouldn't steal anymore.) Discuss with children what they should do when they see something that they want very badly, like the knave who wanted the tarts. What might the knave have done instead?

Help children make crowns for the king, queen, or jack of hearts. Precut heart shapes of various colors and sizes. Have each child glue the hearts to a sentence strip or colorful construction-paper strip, collage style. Collect playing cards or photocopy a king, queen, and jack of hearts from a deck of cards. Children add the appropriate card to their crown collage. When the glue is dry, size the crowns to each child's head and staple to fit. Use the crowns for acting out the rhyme. You can make card costumes for added fun. If you have a poster maker, enlarge the three playing cards to poster size or use an opaque or overhead projector to enlarge the cards onto posterboard. Attach two pieces of posterboard at the top left and right with yarn and have children slip the costumes over their heads.

Have each child make a king or queen's scepter (or just make a single one for the class to use to point to each word as you read your charts). Children cut two heart shapes from construction paper and decorate them with smaller construction-paper hearts, heart stickers, heart-shaped glitter, and what-have-you. Roll a sheet of bond paper on the diagonal from corner to corner to make the stick. Secure with clear tape. Place the stick between the two hearts and staple all three pieces together. Add a few pieces of ribbon if you like, streaming from the end of the heart. Kings and queens need their scepters to rule their kingdoms!

Act out the rhyme. One child will be the knave, one the queen, and another the king. Have each actor wear his or her heart crown (above). The royals might want capes, too (pieces of fabric around the shoulders held in front with clip clothespins) and the king and queen may want thrones (chairs). The queen will need some tarts (pot-pie aluminum pans empty or filled with heart-shaped play dough). As children recite the rhyme, this action takes place.

First verse

Queen pretends to make tarts.

Second verse

Knave sneakily steals the tarts and runs away.

Third verse

King calls for the tarts by clapping twice and then shakes his finger at the knave, saying "No! No! No! Never! Never! Never!"

Last verse

Knave returns the tarts to the queen and bows in apology.
Queen pats the knave on the head in forgiveness.

Look for B. G. Hennessy's *The Missing Tarts* (Viking Kestrel, 1989) illustrated by Tracey Campbell Pearson. In this wonderful story the Queen of Hearts asks different nursery-rhyme characters where her tarts went, and each character answers in rhyme. For example, "Not in my bowl," said Old King Cole. The queen discovers that the knave has given them all away to the children who live in the shoe. Children who are familiar with some of the rhymes will adore this adaptation. Encourage children to write their own stories about what happened to the queen's tarts.

Save the face cards (kings, queens, jacks) from several sets of cards or have parents send some in from decks that are missing cards (every parent has some!). Invite children to sort the royalty by suits, identifying the king of hearts, the queen of hearts, and the jack of hearts and then those of clubs, spades, and diamonds.

Use real cards (if you have enough) or photocopied cards to illustrate the rhyme for individual books that children can take home and "read." You'll also need six "pies" per book, cut from brown or tan construction paper. Fold a large piece of red construction paper into fourths so you have a book with four pages (two fronts and two backs). Computer-generate or write the words for the rhyme on each page and encourage children to glue the appropriate pieces on each page.

Front of book

> The Queen of Hearts,
> She made some tarts,
> All on a summer's day;

queen of hearts card with two
construction-paper pie shapes

Inside left

> The Knave of Hearts,
> He stole the tarts,
> And with them ran away.

jack of hearts card with pie
shapes partially hidden under
the card.

Inside right

> The King of Hearts
> Called for the tarts,
> And scolded the knave full score.

king of hearts card

Back of book

> The Knave of Hearts
> Brought back the tarts,
> And vowed he'd steal no more!

jack of hearts card with two
pie shapes

Play hide and seek with playing cards in the room. Select a student to be the jack and have him or her hide playing-card kings, queens, and jacks. Children hide their eyes and count while the jack is hiding the cards. The child who finds the most cards gets to be the jack.

Photocopy kings, queens, and jacks of hearts from a deck of cards and give children one of each. Have children cut out the cards and glue them to a sheet of white drawing paper. Children use the rectangular shapes as bodies, adding heads, crowns, arms, legs, and so on. Other details from the rhyme can also be added as you encourage children to draw a picture that represents the rhyme.

Add heart-shaped cookie cutters to the play dough area this week. Encourage children to use the heart shapes as bodies and add heads, arms, and legs to make the king, queen, and knave. Heart cookie cutters are easy to find around Valentine's Day or with shape sets of cookie cutters. Children can also make play dough "tarts" by filling a small pie tin with hearts for a heart tart!

Put heart-shaped stencils at your writing table along with scraps of construction paper. Encourage children to use the stencils to draw and cut out heart shapes. Place a large sheet of bulletin-board paper in the area so children can glue their construction-paper hearts to the paper, collage style.

Make the queen's tarts. A tart is a small pie, usually filled with fruit or jam. Give each child a rice cake (plain or flavored) for a tart. Choose plain soft cream cheese and have children use plastic knives or tongue depressors to spread the cream cheese over the rice cake. Add fresh fruit to the top—raisins, slices of apple or banana, strawberries or other berries in season, or whatever fruit is available. Encourage children to design their own tarts and then enjoy. Yum! Or purchase small individual graham-cracker crusts, fill with canned cherry pie filling, and add whipped topping for individual cherry tarts.

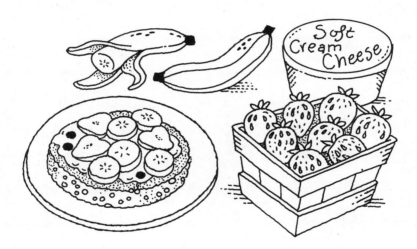

Sing a song of sixpence, a pocketful of rye,
Four-and-twenty blackbirds, baked in a pie;
When the pie was opened, the birds began to sing,
Wasn't that a dainty dish to set before the king?

To introduce this rhyme to your class, photocopy (enlarge if desired) and color the illustration above, mount on a large piece of tagboard, and laminate. Have children predict what they think the rhyme will be about. With the class, label the vocabulary in the picture by drawing lines out from the picture and writing these words in the margins: *sixpence* (an old English coin worth about six pennies), *pie, blackbirds, king.* Children will find other things in the picture to label that do not relate directly to the poem, which is fine.

Go over the words that the class has identified each day, underlining those that relate to the rhyme. Leave out small index cards and encourage children to make their own sight-word flashcards by writing the word on the lined side and illustrating the word on the blank side.

A traditional tune for this nursery rhyme can be found in Pamela Beall and Susan Nipp's *Wee Sing Nursery Rhymes and Lullabies* (Price, Stern & Sloan, 1985). The *Wee Sing* set comes with an audio cassette and sing-along book. It is easily found in most toy, book, or school-supply stores or can be ordered directly from Price, Stern & Sloan Publishers, Inc., 410 North La Cienega Boulevard, Los Angeles, CA 90048.

Randolph Caldecott has illustrated *Sing a Song of Sixpence* (Barron's, 1988) in an old-fashioned, English, line-by-line interpretation. Children will especially enjoy Tracey Campbell Pearson's *Sing a Song of Sixpence* (Dial Books for Young Readers, 1985), which is also a line-by-line illustration of this nursery rhyme. The best thing about this version is that it explains the rhyme in illustrations so that it makes sense! This fanciful book also includes the additional verse about the king in his counting house. Whether or not you read Pearson's book, ask children to explain the rhyme. One possible explanation is that the king's baker paid six cents for some rye to make bread and put the rye in his pocket, which had a hole in it. Some blackbirds followed him to the king's kitchen, eating the rye as it fell from his pocket. When he got to the kitchen, he had all these blackbirds who had followed him, and so for fun, he decided to put them in a pie so that the king could see what his six cents bought! Children will, of course, think up other ways to make sense of the rhyme!

Practice counting from 1 to 24 by ones and then by twos—both orally and with written numbers. Have each child make a set of 24, using anything in the room—pencils, paper clips, rubber bands, wooden blocks, and so on.

Write the rhyme on sentence strips and then cut each word apart. Use the individual words to make a graph. Write the numerals 1 through 10 in a line at the bottom of the chalkboard. Put a piece of double-sided tape on the back of each word. Have children count the number of letters in each word and put the word card above the number that represents its total number of letters. Discuss the graph. Which number has the most words? Which word(s) is the longest? the shortest? Which numbers have no words?

Use the cut-apart words as sight-word flashcards, or challenge small groups or individual children to put the rhyme back together on the floor or in a pocket chart.

Help children make a bulletin board or mural for this rhyme. Lay one child down on a large sheet of white bulletin board paper and trace around his or her body. Children fill in the clothes and features with poster paint. Add a king's crown cut from construction paper—several children can help glue sequins and glitter to the crown. When it is dry, glue the crown to the king's head. Have another group of volunteers cut a pie shape from brown construction paper. Cut a slit in the top of the "pie" and fold the paper back. Trace around each child's hands (thumb out, fingers together) on black construction paper. Cut out and glue together with thumbs on top of each other to make blackbirds. Wiggly eyes or two white paper reinforcements can be added for eyes. Glue the "birds" coming out of the top of the "pie."

For children who need practice with colors or color words, change the color word in the language chunk . . . *four-and-twenty* black*birds baked in a pie* . . . and make a class book. Have children use stencils to trace and cut brown or tan pie shapes for each page. Cut a slit at the top of each pie and fold out so that the birds look like they are coming

out of the pie. On each page, write the line with a different color word, such as . . . *four-and-twenty* red *birds baked in a pie*. Have a child or children working in small groups draw with markers, sponge-paint, trace stencils and cut from construction paper, or simply glue 24 precut bird shapes of the appropriate color coming out of the pie on each page. Assemble the pages into a class book.

...four and twenty black birds baked in a pie.

 Cut pie shapes for your flannel board from tan or brown felt. Write the numerals 1 to 10 (or 24!) on each pie shape with permanent marker. Cut simple blackbird shapes from black felt. Children can place the correct number of birds over each pie. Or make this into a game by using small aluminum pie tins with round felt "pie-crust" covers. Write a number inside each pie tin. Have children use small black feathers as counters (available with craft supplies) to count the appropriate number of black feathers into each pie and cover it with a "pie crust."

Show the class Bernard Most's *Four and Twenty Dinosaurs*. This is a collection of nursery rhymes with dinosaurs replacing the main characters, and the cover features "Dinosaur Pie!" The rhyme is later illustrated in the text. This fanciful illustration may give children other ideas for things to bake in a pie. Have each child fill in the sentence: King or Queen (child's name's) pie is full of four-and-twenty _____. Write their completed sentences at the bottom of sheets of drawing paper and have children illustrate their sentences. Have a volunteer draw the cover and add the title "Four-and-Twenty Blackbirds Baked in a Pie." Display on a bulletin board and later assemble into a class book.

Have children brainstorm possible names for the king and vote on their favorite.

Read Francis Reid's *Sing a Song of Mother Goose* (Scholastic, 1991), which is a collection of nursery rhymes that includes "Sing a Song of Sixpence," "Old King Cole," and "Humpty Dumpty." This collection has wonderful illustrations sculpted in clay.

King and Queen Activities

Make a castle from a refrigerator box. Invite children to help you with the design. Draw an outline with a pencil and cut along the lines with a mat knife. Make sure you have a door that opens. Take the box outside so that the children can help you paint it. Add some glitter while the paint is wet to give the castle a little extra sparkle. After the paint is dry, add some flourishes with gold or silver spray paint. Use the castle for play or as a quiet reading nook.

Children will enjoy the wonderfully illustrated *Castles: A First Discovery Book* by Gallimard Jeunesse and others (Cartwheel Books/Scholastic, 1990), which gives an inside view of castle life.

Encourage children to make castles with the building supplies in your classroom. You might even consider purchasing special plastic "castle" blocks. To encourage play, add paper crowns to any small toy people that you have. Children enjoy the castle play and acting out the rhymes with the building supplies.

Encourage children to make crowns to wear around the room from any flexible manipulatives that you might have in the room, such as Flexiblocks, loops, strings, and large wooden beads.

Make king and queen crowns for each child from sentence strips or from two strips of construction paper stapled together. Cut into crown shapes and have children add anything that sparkles—sequins, shiny ribbon, glitter, foil bits, foil wrapping-paper pieces, or gummed foil stars. To collect the sparkly stuff, ask parents to send in one item of their choice, such as a bag of silver sequins, a package of shiny gummed stars, skinny silver ribbon, gold wrapping paper, or silver glitter. Size crowns to children's heads and staple. Or ask Burger King for crowns to embellish.

Younger students will enjoy the 40-minute video *Barney's Magical Musical Adventure* (Lyons Group, Inc.) which features Old King Cole, a "Tea Party Medley" that includes "Sing a Song of Sixpence," and an array of other castle adventures.

More mature students will enjoy the 60-minute Wee Sing video *King Cole's Party* (Price, Stern & Sloan, 1987). This video uses real people to act out nursery rhymes in a story format. The main plot centers on the people of the kingdom coming to King Cole's birthday party. The video includes many of the rhymes included in *Hang Loose, Mother Goose!*

Children will enjoy this activity after they have memorized several nursery rhymes. Select any collection of nursery rhymes and show children each page, asking "Do we know this rhyme?" This will help teach children the importance of looking for picture clues as they read. If they say no, turn the page until children identify a rhyme they recognize. *Every* collection includes "Humpty Dumpty"! Continue all the way through the collection. Select a different one each day.

Make an audio cassette to go with this unit, including songs recorded commercially as well as individual children and the class reciting and singing each of the rhymes.

Make a class video of children acting out "Humpty Dumpty," "Old King Cole," and "The Queen of Hearts." Send the video home with a different child each night so that families can enjoy it. Or invite parents in to be "kings and queens for a day." Send crown-shaped invitations, serve the queen's tarts (made by the children, of course) and have children act out the rhymes or show the video. Be sure each child is included.

Ask children to brainstorm a list of popular stories about royalty. Disney has a fondness for royalty, so start with these: *Cinderella, Snow White, Aladdin, Sleeping Beauty, The Little Mermaid*. Identify the king and queen in each story and discuss what part they play. Ask your librarian about the array of other books that feature castles and royalty.

CAT AND MOUSE RHYMES

Hickory Dickory Dock
Three Blind Mice
Three Little Kittens
Pussycat, Pussycat

Hickory Dickory Dock

Hickory dickory dock,
The mouse ran up the clock.
The clock struck one
And down he did run.
Hickory dickory dock!

Both Marilyn Janowitz's *Hickory Dickory Dock* (Hyperion Books for Children, 1991) and Moira Kemp's *Hickory Dickory Dock* (Dutton/Lodestar Children's Books, 1991) illustrate the rhyme line-by-line in delightful renditions.

A traditional tune for this nursery rhyme can be found in Pamela Beall and Susan Nipp's *Wee Sing Nursery Rhymes and Lullabies* (Price, Stern & Sloan, 1985). The *Wee Sing* set comes with an audio cassette and sing-along book. It is easily found in most toy, book, or school-supply stores or can be ordered directly from Price, Stern & Sloan Publishers, Inc., 410 North La Cienega Boulevard, Los Angeles, CA 90048.

Try singing or saying the rhyme v-e-r-y s-l-o-w-ly and then very, very fast. Sing it once through very loudly and then whisper it softly. Sing the song in a very low "Daddy Mouse" voice, in a higher-pitched "Mommy Mouse" voice, and finally in a wee little "Baby Mouse" voice. Children will enjoy playing with their voices and will get lots of practice memorizing the rhyme!

Try the following body movements to reinforce the words of this rhyme.

Hickory dickory dock,	Bend side-to-side three times with hands on hips.
The mouse ran up the clock.	Run two fingers up opposite arm.
The clock struck one	Index finger pointing straight up.
And down he did run.	Run two fingers quickly down other side.
Hickory dickory dock!	Bend side-to-side three times with hands on hips.

Another fun way to teach this rhyme is to add the words *tick tock*. Teach the rhyme the following way.

Hickory dickory dock, (tick tock)

The mouse ran up the clock. (tick tock)

The clock struck one

And down he did run.

Hickory dickory dock! (tick tock)

Children love saying "tick tock." Divide the class into two groups and have one group say the lines and the other group say the tick tocks.

Create some props to help children act out this rhyme. Make a grandfather clock by enlarging one from an illustration of the rhyme. Attach it to the wall or to a large box so that it is self-standing. Look for a mouse finger puppet or a stuffed mouse, or make a laminated construction-paper mouse to use. Invite a child to manipulate the mouse around the clock as the other children say the rhyme. Leave the props out for children to use independently.

 Help children make props that they can use to act out the rhyme by themselves. Clocks can be made from small paper plates with numbers written around the perimeter. Have each child use a tagboard stencil to draw and then cut a grandfather-clock shape from brown construction paper. (This can be as simple as a large rectangle. Be sure that the width is slightly wider than that of the paper plate.) Attach two construction-paper hands to each paper-plate clock with a brass fastener. Have children make mice by cutting hearts from construction paper. When folded in half and glued together, the point of the heart becomes the mouse's nose. Add a small pompom for the nose, two construction-paper circles for the ears (one on each side) and plastic wiggle eyes. Use yarn for the tail. Encourage children to use their props to act out the rhyme and then take the props home to share with their families.

Hickory Dickory Dock
The mouse ran up the clock
The clock struck one
And down he did run
Hickory Dickory Dock

Children will also enjoy acting out this rhyme without props. Use the children themselves as props—one child as the clock and another the mouse. The clock says, "Tick, tock, tick, tock . . ." and then uses his or her arms like clock arms to make one o'clock. The mouse pretends to climb up the side of the clock slowly, jumps at one o'clock, and then scurries away in a hurry. Have the "audience" say the rhyme as two children act it out. Guide timid actors as needed.

Write the rhyme on a sheet of chart paper and laminate. Instead of words, substitute the pictures of the clock and mouse on pages 268 and 270 or create your own. Point to each word as you read. When you come to a picture, stop and have children supply the word. Write *clock* and *mouse* twice each on sticky notes and have children match the words with the pictures on the chart.

 Make a mouse pointer (place a stuffed, plastic, or rubber mouse or a mouse cut from laminated construction paper or fun foam at the end of a dowel) to encourage the children to point to each word as they "read." Leave the pointer out to encourage children to "read" individually.

 Use the laminated chart each day. Have children come up to the chart and circle words, letters, or punctuation that you identify (periods, commas, capital letters, rhyming words, and so on) with washable markers.

 Underline the words *clock* and *dock* on the laminated rhyme chart. Have children brainstorm a list of words with the *-ock* ending, such as *lock*, *sock*, *block*, *rock*, and *knock*. Keep the list up and add to it as children think of new words. At the end of the week, have children make their own "Rhyming Clock" book by choosing some words to illustrate—one word to a page.

Cut two covers from gray construction paper and three pages from white paper in a mouse shape to make a rhyme book as follows. This sequencing of the rhyme will help children remember it. Be sure children take the book home to "read" to their families.

Page 1

Hickory dickory dock (written by children or preprinted for very young children)

Page 2

The mouse ran up the clock. (picture of mouse climbing *up* clock)

Page 3

The clock struck one, (picture of a clock showing 1:00)

Page 4

And down he did run. (picture of mouse running *down* clock)

Page 5

Hickory dickory dock! (written by children or preprinted for very young children)

Make a class book by having volunteers make clocks showing each hourly time from 1:00 to 12:00. Children may use circle stencils or rubber stamps, or add hands to clock notepad sheets (available from Carson-Dellosa and Shapes, Etc.) for similar-looking clocks. Or you can encourage them to draw different kinds of clocks, such as grandfather clocks, alarm clocks, digital clocks, and so on. At the bottom of the first page, write the words

Hickory dickory dock
The mouse ran up the clock.
The clock struck one.

Change the number in the verse on each following page. Sequence the pages from 1 to 12. Draw a little mouse on the cover and add the title, "Time Will Tell." You can also have children make individual books to take home. Preprint the words for the pages, leaving out the numerals, and have children draw clocks on each page.

Invite children to say the rhyme with you. Tell them that when the mouse gets to the top of the clock, they will hear a bell ring to indicate the hour. Ring the bell a different number of times each time you say the rhyme and challenge the class to count the chimes.

Hickory dickory dock,

The mouse ran up the clock.

The clock struck _____ (Ring bell a certain number of times and have children call out the number.)

And down he did run.

Hickory dickory dock!

Or use the rhyme and have children take turns filling in the number. When a leader says the number, children clap, snap, or jump up and down the appropriate number of times.

Jim Aylesworth's *The Completed Hickory Dickory Dock* (Atheneum, 1990) illustrated by Eileen Christelow, starts with the traditional rhyme and then adds another verse for each number up to 12:00. Children love this book and may be inspired to write (or sing!) some versions of their own.

 This is a good rhyme for telling-time practice. Set up a clock center in your classroom. Ask parents to send in clocks that no longer work for children to play with—wind-up alarm clocks, old watches, electric clocks, stopwatches, digital clocks, and so on. Take the back off one of the clocks so children can observe all the parts inside (be careful with small parts and very young children). Add a teaching clock with movable hands, such as the Judy clock, a large wooden clock with movable hands that children can manipulate. (Judy/Instructo also has a giant clock floor puzzle and individual smaller clocks.) Add a clock-shaped rubber stamp and paper to the center and encourage children to add hands and numbers.

Make a clock snack. Use a flavored rice cake or large bakery-style sugar cookie for each child. Children use plastic knives or tongue depressors to spread cream cheese (plain or flavored) over their rice cakes. Add 12 raisins or chocolate chips to represent the numbers on the clock. Demonstrate for the class how to put one chip at 12:00, one at 6:00, one at 9:00, and one at 3:00. This helps with spacing. Children can then add the rest of the raisins. Give each child one short and one long thin carrot stick or licorice string to use as clock hands. Demonstrate placing the "hands" at 1:00. Eat and enjoy!

Look for *Hickory Dickory Pizza Clock* by Mark Buelleo (Celebration Press/Scott Foresman, 1996), a small book for emergent readers that describes the steps for making a pizza clock. The book starts with the rolled-out dough, then adds sauce and cheese. Pepperoni slices form numbers 12, 3, 6, and 9, and small black olive slices fill in the rest. Slices of bell pepper make the long and short hands. Have children read the book and then make this delicious pizza clock! Take photographs of the children as they make the clock and sequence the pictures to make your own class "Hickory Dickory Pizza Clock" book.

Children will also enjoy books about clocks and time during the study of this rhyme. As you introduce each book, have children identify the front and back of the book. Point out the title page, the author's name, the illustrator's name, and so on. Look for some of the following books about clocks and time.

Hutchins, Pat. *Clocks and More Clocks*. Macmillan, 1994.

Katz, Bobbi. *Tick Tock, Let's Read the Clock*. Random House, 1988.

Kelly, Donna. *The Clock Book*. Western Publishing Company, 1978.

Llewellyn, Claire. *My First Book of Time*. Dorling Kindersley, 1992.

Maestro, Betsy and Giulio. *Around the Clock With Harriet*. Crown, 1984.

McMillan, Bruce. *Time To . . . .* Lothrop, Lee & Shepard, 1989.

Potter, Beatrix. *What Time Is It, Peter Rabbit?* F. Warne & Company, 1989.

Rockwell, Anne. *Bear Child's Book of Hours*. Thomas J. Crowell, 1987.

Warren, Cathy. *The Ten-Alarm Camp-out*. Lothrop, Lee & Shepard, 1983.

Youlder, Gillian. *Time*. Franklin Watts, 1979.

Have a "Hickory Dickory Dock" snack by helping children make mice. Give each child a canned or fresh pear half, cut vertically. Lay each pear half flat side down on a plate. Use round slices of banana for ears and half slices for feet. Use a sliver of celery, carrot, or licorice string for the mouse's tail. Shoestring licorice or thinly-sliced cheese makes nice whiskers. Cut a small triangle from red fruit roll for a nose and use donut-shaped cereal pieces for two beady eyes.

Write numerals 1 through 5 or 1 through 10 down the left side of a sheet of white paper. Have children make the appropriate number of thumbprints beside each number by using a black washable ink pad. Show them how to turn each thumbprint into a little mouse by adding two ears, two eyes, and a tail with a thin black marker or pen. A mouse rubber stamp can also be used to stamp the appropriate number of mice beside each numeral.

Consider adopting a mouse as a class pet. They can be purchased inexpensively from most pet stores. Or ask a pet-store owner to bring in a mouse for show-and-tell, along with some interesting facts about mice. Children will enjoy *Mouse Views: What the Class Pet Saw* by Bruce McMillan (Holiday House, 1993). This guessing-game book shows pictures of the classroom from a mouse's viewpoint and encourages children to try to guess what they are seeing.

"Hickory Dickory Dock" is thought to have originated as a "counting-out" or "choosing" rhyme and can be used for choosing a leader. The teacher points to a child on each word as the rhyme is said. A child is eliminated if the teacher says "dock" or "clock" when pointing to that child. The one left is the chosen one. Use this to decide who your line leader is for the day or any time you need to choose one child for a task. It provides great reinforcement of the rhyme.

 Read *No Hickory No Dickory No Dock* by John Agard and Grace Nichols (Candlewick Press, 1991) to your class. This is a collection of nursery rhymes with a Caribbean/West Indies flair. The book is worth the single innovation of "Hickory Dickory Dock" in which a mouse says that he didn't do it! Copy this poem on chart paper and use it as the centerpiece for a bulletin board of handmade mice or clocks.

Read *Hickory Dickory Dock and Other Nursery Rhymes*, beautifully illustrated by Carol Jones (Houghton Mifflin, 1992). "Hickory Dickory Dock" is the first rhyme in this collection. Children especially enjoy this book because each additional rhyme has the little mouse from "Hickory Dickory Dock" disguised in its illustration for children to find.

Three blind mice, three blind mice.
See how they run. See how they run.
They all ran after the farmer's wife,
Who cut off their tails with a carving knife.
Have you ever seen such a sight in your life
As three blind mice?

 Introduce this rhyme to children with turn-of-the-century British writer John W. Ivimey's complete poem, which was inspired by the well-loved Mother Goose rhyme. Ivimey's words have been cleverly illustrated by Victoria Chess in *Three Blind Mice* (Joy Street Books, 1990) and by Paul Galdone in *Three Blind Mice* (Clarion, 1987). Both editions include the music for the nursery-rhyme tune. These updated versions are especially endearing because they expand on the original rhyme to include how the mice became blind, what happened to the farmer's wife, and how the mice's tails grew back. It keeps children from being concerned that the farmer's wife was so violent!

Find a picture of the rhyme to show children and mount it on tagboard. Ask what they think is happening in the picture. With the class, label the vocabulary in the picture (*blind mice, farmer's wife, carving knife, tails*). Children will find other things to label that do not relate directly to the poem, which is fine. Go over the words that the class has identified each day, pointing out those that specifically relate to the rhyme.

Read one complete line of the rhyme, pointing to each word on a chart as you recite. Have children echo the line back to you as you point to each word. Divide the class into two groups. One side "reads" a line and the other side echoes it. Have groups take turns being line readers and echoers.

Help children make props and act out the rhyme. Mouse ears can be made by cutting two large circles from gray construction paper. Add smaller pink construction paper circles to the insides of each ear or use pink paint. Attach the ears to headbands made from strips of gray construction paper or pink sentence strips stapled to size for each head. Use the ears, three pairs of sunglasses (look for sunglasses sold as party favors), and three pieces of rope or ribbon for each mouse tail (tucked in at the waist of pants or skirts). The farmer's wife chases the mice and pulls off their tails instead of cutting them with a knife.

Make a set of mouse ears and a tail for each child to wear home. Optional: add whiskers and a little black upside-down triangle nose with an eyeliner pencil or black tempera or acrylic paint, which will not rub off. Parents are sure to ask what children learned at school that day! This gives them a chance to practice the rhyme at home.

Write the rhyme on chart paper and laminate. Call out words and letters and have individuals come up and circle the words or letters with a wipe-off marker. For example, they might underline words or phrases that are the same, circle rhyming words, or draw a box around periods or capital letters. Have children count the number of words in each line or in the entire rhyme.

At the play dough center, have children practice making mouse tails by rolling the play dough into snakes and ropes. They can use a "carving knife" (plastic knife, tongue depressor, or craft stick) to cut the tails.

 Enjoy Ed Young's *Seven Blind Mice* (Philomel, 1992) about a different set of mice and their adventures (an innovation of the traditional story "The Blind Men and the Elephant"). This book may encourage children to write their own adventures about different numbers of mice. Display students' mouse adventures with the title, "Mouse Tails."

 Play "pin the tail on the mouse" in the same way that you play pin the tail on the donkey. Blow up a picture of a profile of a mouse on posterboard and stick pieces of tape on the ends of ribbons for the tails. Blindfold children, turn them around three times, and then let them try to place the tail on the mouse. The child whose tail is closest gets to give a treat (a small block of cheese!) to the other children.

 Teach children to play this version of blind man's buff. Have children form a circle with one blindfolded child in the middle. As you turn the "blind man" around three times, have the children in the circle hold hands and walk clockwise, chanting the following verse.

> Blind man, blind man,
>
> Sure you can't see?
>
> Turn around three times
>
> And try to catch me!

When the chant is finished, children "freeze." The blind man walks until he or she touches a child and tries to identify that child by feeling the child's face. He or she continues until a child is identified. Then that child becomes the blind man. (It's easy to identify most children because they just can't help giggling!)

 A mouse's favorite snack is cheese, so serve bite-size pieces of cheese for snack with crackers or apple slices. For a cheese-tasting party, ask parents to send in samples of different types of cheese and have the children graph which they like the best!

111

Have each child dictate a story to a parent volunteer or older child that explains how Swiss cheese got its holes.

Mice are main characters in much of children's literature. As you read a book to the class, point out the front and back of the book, the title page, the name of the author, and that of the illustrator. Check your own library or select some of the following age-appropriate books about mice.

Baker, Alan. *Two Tiny Mice*. Dial, 1991.

Baker, Alan. *Where's Mouse?* Kingfisher, 1992.

Brett, Jan. *Town Mouse, Country Mouse*. G. P. Putnam's Sons, 1994.

Carle, Eric. *Do You Want to Be My Friend?* PLB, 1971.

Dunbar, Joyce. *Ten Little Mice*. Harcourt Brace Jovanovich, 1990.

Fisher, Aileen. *The House of a Mouse*. HarperCollins, 1988.

Fleming, Denise. *Lunch*. Henry Holt and Company, 1992.

Freeman, Don. *Norman the Doorman*. Puffin, 1981.

Holabird, Katherine. *Angelina Ballerina*. Crown, 1988. (Look for other Angelina adventures.)

Kraus, Robert. *Come Out and Play, Little Mouse*. Mulberry Books, 1995.

Lionni, Leo. *Frederick*. Pantheon, 1967. (Look for other Leo Lionni mouse tales.)

Lobel, Arnold. *Mouse Tales*. Harper and Row, 1972. (Available with audio cassette: Caedmon, 1990.)

Numeroff, Laura Joffe. *If You Give a Mouse a Cookie*. HarperCollins, 1994.

Walsh, Ellen Stoll. *Mouse Count*. Harcourt Brace Jovanovich, 1991.

Walsh, Ellen Stoll. *Mouse Paint*. Harcourt Brace Jovanovich, 1989.

Wood, Don and Audrey. *The Little Mouse, the Red Ripe Strawberry and the Big Hungry Bear*. Child's Play Ltd., 1990.

The three little kittens, they lost their mittens
And they began to cry,
"Oh, Mother dear, we sadly fear,
Our mittens we have lost!"

"What? Lost your mittens, you naughty kittens?
Then you shall have no pie.
Meow, meow, meow!
Then you shall have no pie!"

The three little kittens, they found their mittens
And they began to cry,
"Oh, Mother dear, see here, see here,
Our mittens we have found!"

"What? Found your mittens, you good little kittens?
Then you shall have some pie!
Meow, meow, meow
Then you shall have some pie!"

"Purr, purr, purr.
Sh-h-h. I smell a mouse close by!

A traditional tune for this nursery rhyme can be found in Pamela Beall and Susan Nipp's *Wee Sing Nursery Rhymes and Lullabies* (Price, Stern & Sloan, 1985). The *Wee Sing* set comes with an audio cassette and sing-along book. It is easily found in most toy, book, or school-supply stores or can be ordered directly from Price, Stern & Sloan Publishers, Inc., 410 North La Cienega Boulevard, Los Angeles, CA 90048.

Paul Galdone's *Three Little Kittens* (Clarion Books, 1986) has excellent illustrations for this classic rhyme. Lilian Obligado's older *Three Little Kittens* (Random House, 1974) and Lorinda Cauley's *Three Little Kittens* (Putnam, 1982) also illustrate the rhyme line-by-line.

Make a "Three Kittens' Pie" snack with children. Use any prepared pie mix or your own favorite recipe.

After children have learned this nursery rhyme, help them act it out. One child is the mother cat and three children are kittens. Don't forget to have one child be a mouse for the last line. You may wish to add props, but children can act it out without them. Use an apron for the mother cat (cut from a white plastic garbage bag), a pie tin for a pretend pie, and real mittens. Make simple mouse ears (see page 110) for the mouse and cat ears for the cat and kittens (hot-glue black felt triangles to inexpensive black headbands and add a little pink felt to the middle of each). You are the narrator. Encourage characters to say as much of their part of the verse as possible, even if you have to prompt them as you go along.

 Write this rhyme on chart paper and laminate, using the illustrations on pages 268–272 for some of the key words (*kitten, three, mittens, pie*). When you come to these words, stop and let children say them. Write the words on sticky notes and encourage children to match words and pictures.

 Make a pointer stick by hot-gluing a cat with plastic wiggle eyes cut from construction paper or black fun foam (or look for small black plastic or stuffed cats around Halloween) to the end of a dowel. Use the cat pointer as you read the rhyme chart in the above activity. Point to individual words randomly from the chart and see if children can name them. Leave the pointer out for individual students to use as they "read" the rhyme.

Each day have children come up to the laminated chart and identify concepts you select, using a washable marker. For example, they might circle the quotation marks, underline what the mother cat says, underline words with short vowel sounds, circle rhyming words, and so on.

Make a class book for children who need help identifying colors or color words. Have each child draw his or her full body with both arms and hands showing. Precut some mitten shapes or have children cut them using stencils—two mitten shapes of each color. Have children glue the colored mittens at the end of their hands—one over each hand. At the bottom of each page, write (*Child's name*) *found his or her (color) mittens!* Bind these together in a class book. On the cover, use a picture of the three little kittens with their mittens and title it "The Three Little Kittens Found Their Mittens!"

Symphonie found her yellow mittens.

 As you go through each page of the book in the above activity, identify colors using the following song, sung to the tune of "Mary Had a Little Lamb."

Jimmy found his red mittens, red mittens, red mittens
Jimmy found his red mittens
They were on his hands!

Use cat- or mitten-shaped note pads (available from Shapes, Etc. or Carson-Dellosa) or cut cat and mitten shapes from construction paper (use cookie cutters or Ellison dies) to use as number flashcards. After children say the numeral on the flash card, have them meow the appropriate number of times, using fingers to keep count. Have them identify the number that comes before and after the flashed number. Make other sets of flashcards to identify alphabet letters, sight words, Dolch words, spelling words, number words, colors, and color words.

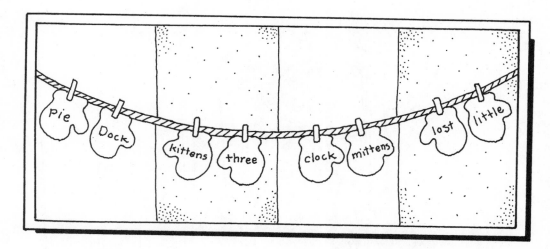

Run a clothesline across the room. In the middle of the clothesline, pin the title, "Kittens' Clothesline." On the clothesline, use clip clothespins to pin words from this unit written on mitten shapes. Write rhyming words on matching colored mittens. Using the clothesline, play games with children, such as: find a word with three letters, find a word that rhymes with _____, find a word from the "Hickory Dickory Dock" nursery rhyme, find a word with a capital letter, find a word that means _____, or find a word that begins with the k sound.

Look for cat- and mitten-shaped cookie cutters to use with play dough. Cats are easy to find around Halloween, and mittens are usually found in December and January. The open-frame variety of cookie cutter works well. Add pie tins so that children can make mother cat's pie.

Pussycat, pussycat, where have you been?
"I've been to London to visit the Queen."
Pussycat, pussycat, what did you there?
"I frightened a little mouse under her chair."

A traditional tune for this nursery rhyme can be found in Pamela Beall and Susan Nipp's *Wee Sing Nursery Rhymes and Lullabies* (Price, Stern & Sloan, 1985). The *Wee Sing* set comes with an audio cassette and sing-along book. It is easily found in most toy, book, or school-supply stores or can be ordered directly from Price, Stern & Sloan Publishers, Inc., 410 North La Cienega Boulevard, Los Angeles, CA 90048.

To help students understand this rhyme, show them London and England on a map or globe. Have students find pictures of Queen Elizabeth or former kings and queens in all their royal garb so that they will understand the setting of the poem.

Look for a picture of this rhyme or use the illustration on page 118. Photocopy (enlarge if you wish), color, and mount the picture on tagboard. Have children identify important vocabulary in the picture (*pussycat, queen, mouse, chair*). Then draw a line out from each word to the margin and write the word. Children will identify some things that are not pertinent to the rhyme, which is fine.

To act out this rhyme, you will need one child to be the queen on her throne, one child to be the cat, and a third child to be the mouse. You don't need props but they help young children visualize the scene. You might use a crown for the queen. A sheet makes a nice robe that can be clothespinned Batman-style at the neck. Make cat ears and mouse ears on headbands (see pages 110 and 115). You act as narrator, and the cat says the words that are answers ("I've been to London to visit the queen" and "I frightened a little mouse under her chair"). The cat then chases the mouse while the queen faints!

Write the rhyme on chart paper and laminate. Have children come up each day to circle letters or words and language conventions with a washable marker. For example, you might have them look for words that have the *k* sound at the beginning (discuss *c* and *k*), quotation marks, capital letters, periods, and so on. Children can underline rhyming words. Have the class brainstorm a list of words that rhyme with *chair* and *there* (*bear, pear, tear, wear, care, dare, hare, mare, rare, stare, spare, fair, hair, lair, pair, stair*). Discuss how these word endings are spelled differently but sound the same.

Read *Red Cat White Cat* by Peter Mandel (Henry Holt & Company, 1994) to the class. This "Bill Martin Book" is a simple book of opposites. After reading the book, have children come up with other opposites, such as big cat/little cat, fat cat/thin cat, hairy cat/bald cat (or have children illustrate colored cats, such as red cat/purple cat/brown cat). Have volunteers illustrate each of the concepts and compile illustrations into a class big book. Use a paw-shaped rubber stamp from a felt-tipped marker set for the cover, much like the opening pages of *Red Cat White Cat*.

 After making the big book, use the opposites to illustrate the language chunk, *Pussycat, pussycat, where have you been?* Substitute some of the opposites for the underlined words (*Big cat, big cat, where have you been?*). Make sticky notes of the opposites and have children place them over the appropriate words on the laminated chart. With the class, read the new rhymes, incorporating the words on the sticky notes.

 There are at least two different collections of cat nursery rhymes that children will enjoy with this unit: Barbara Lucas' *Cats by Mother Goose* (Lothrop, Lee & Shepard, 1986) and Robin Michael Koontz's *Pussycat Ate the Dumplings: Cat Rhymes From Mother Goose* (Dodd, Mead, 1987). Have each child select a favorite cat nursery rhyme to write on the bottom of a piece of drawing paper. Have them illustrate the rhyme at the top.

There are many, many books for this age group that feature cats and kittens as the main characters. Also included in this list are some nonfiction books about cats and kittens. As you read a book to the class, identify the front and back of the book, have children predict what they think each book will be about from the cover illustration, and identify the author and the illustrator. Ask your librarian for some popular selections or choose from the following list.

Abercrombie, Barbara. *Michael and the Cats*. Macmillan Children's Group, 1993.

Allen, Pamela. *My Cat Maisie*. Viking, 1991.

Astley, Judy. *When One Cat Woke Up: A Cat Counting Book*. Dial Books, 1990.

Balian, Lorna. *Amelia's Nine Lives*. Humbug Books, 1986.

Bryant, Donna. *My Cat Buster*. Barron, 1991.

Burns, Theresa. *You're Not My Cat*. HarperCollins, 1989.

Carle, Eric. *Have You Seen My Cat?* Picture Book Studio, 1991.

Charles, Donald. *Calico Cat at School*. Childrens Press, 1981. (Look for other books in this series.)

Cherry, Lynne. *Archie, Follow Me*. Dutton, 1990.

Christensen, Nancy. *Good Night, Little Kitten*. Childrens Press, 1990.

DeRegniers, Beatrice S. *It Does Not Say Meow and Other Animal Rhymes*. Clarion, 1972.

DeRegniers, Beatrice S. *So Many Cats!* Clarion Books, 1985.

Dr. Seuss. *The Cat in the Hat*. Random House Books for Young Readers, 1987.

Dr. Seuss. *The Cat in the Hat Comes Back*. Random House, 1958.

Fowler, Allan. *It Could Still Be a Cat*. Childrens Press, 1993.

Gag, Wanda. *Millions of Cats*. Coward, 1928.

Galdone, Paul. *Cat Goes Fiddle-i-Fee*. Houghton Mifflin, 1985.

Hoban, Tana. *One Little Kitten*. Greenwillow, 1979.

James, Betsy. *He Wakes Me*. Orchard Books, 1991.

Kellogg, Steven. *A Rose for Pinkerton*. Dial, 1981.

Kettner, Christine. *An Ordinary Cat*. HarperCollins, 1991.

Lear, Edward. *The Owl and the Pussycat*. Houghton Mifflin, 1989.

Lehman, Martin. *Ten Cats and Their Tales*. Holt, 1982.

Lewin, Betsy. *Cat Count*. Dodd, Mead and Company, 1981.

Moore, Inga. *Six-Dinner Sid*. Simon & Schuster, 1993.

Mortimer, Anne. *Tosca's Surprise*. Puffin, 1994.

Petty, Kate. *First Pets: Cats*. Barron, 1993.

Polushkin, Maria. *Here's That Kitten!* Bradbury Press, 1990.

Polushkin, Maria. *Kitten in Trouble*. Bradbury Press, 1986.

Reiser, Lynn. *Bedtime Cat*. Greenwillow, 1991.

Rose, Agatha. *Hide-and-Seek in the Yellow House*. Viking, 1992.

Scamell, Ragnhild. *Solo Plus One*. Little, 1992.

Sneed, Bard. *Lucky Russell*. Putnam, 1992.

Wahl, Jan. *My Cat Ginger*. Morrow, 1992.

Ward, Cindy. *Cookie's Week*. G. P. Putnam's Sons, 1988.

Weihs, Erika. *Count on Cats*. Doubleday, 1976.

Wildsmith, Brian. *The Cat Sat on the Mat*. Oxford University Press, 1982.

Zeifert, Harriet. *Cat Games*. Puffin, 1988.

Zeifert, Harriet. *Dr. Cat*. Puffin, 1989.

Look for pictures of cats in magazines, and have children cut out pictures that they find (you might want to have some precut). Children can glue all the cat pictures to a large piece of tagboard to make a group cat collage. Add a poem about cats selected from *Maynard's Dream* by David S. Rose (Atheneum, 1991).

Invite a cat lover into your classroom. A local pet store or the Humane Society may have some suggestions. The pet owner should be able to discuss different kinds of cats and cat care. Ask the speaker to bring a calm, declawed cat that children can touch and stroke. Take instant photographs of the children with the cat. Display the photos with this nursery rhyme (you can substitute *this little cat* for *pussy*).

I love little pussy, her coat is so warm,

And if I don't hurt her, she'll do me no harm.

I'll sit by the fire and give her some food,

And pussy will love me because I am good.

Call your local animal shelter and ask about supplies that can be donated for the cats there, such as food and treats. Encourage each child in your class to make a donation or have the class lead a drive for supplies at your school. Arrange a field trip to the animal shelter to deliver the goods.

Cat and Mouse Activities

Read the following nursery rhyme to the class. Have children act it out and then discuss why the mice don't want the cat to come in.

Six little mice sat down to spin.

Pussy passed by and she peeped in.

"What are you doing, my little men?"

"Weaving coats for gentlemen."

"Shall I come in and cut off your threads?"

"No, no Mistress Pussy, you'd bite off our heads."

"Oh no, I'll not: I'll help you to spin."

"That may be so, but do not come in!"

To follow up on the above rhyme, cut coat shapes from plastic needlepoint canvas. Purchase a large, blunt needlepoint needle or a plastic needle and show children how to lace around the edges or make crisscrosses all over the coat shapes.

Make Cat and Mouse Counting Books. Give each child a booklet with blank pages. Have children write a number from 1 to 10 or from 1 to 20 on each page, or have them find the numbers in magazines and cut them out.

Show children how to draw a cat.

Draw a large circle for a body and a smaller circle on top for a head. Add two triangle ears and a tail. Add eyes, a mouth, a nose, and whiskers.

Then teach them how to draw a mouse.

Draw a circle for the head, two small circle ears, dots for eyes and an upside-down triangle for the nose. Add whiskers.

Invite children to draw the appropriate number of cats or mice on each page of their counting books.

To understand the adversarial relationship of cats and mice, watch some Tom and Jerry cartoons with children. Tom is a cat who is always trying to catch Jerry, and Jerry is a mouse who is always trying to outsmart Tom!

Encourage the children to play cat and mouse outside, with one child as the cat and the other children as the mice. Use the same rules as for chase or hide-and-seek.

Teach children this adaptation of a traditional fingerplay with motions about mice running from a cat.

Five little mice standing in a row,	Hold up five fingers.
They nod their heads to the children so.	Bend wrist.
They run to the left; they run to the right.	Wiggle fingers to right and then to left.
They stand up and stretch in the bright sunlight.	Stretch hand above head.
Along comes a cat who's in for some fun.	Move other fist toward fingers.
MEOW! See those little mice run!	Move fingers fast behind back.

This is another traditional rhyme with motions.

Five little mice on the pantry floor.	Hold up five fingers.
This little mouse peeked behind the door;	Bend thumb.
This little mouse nibbled at some cake;	Bend down pointer finger.
This little mouse not a sound did make;	Bend down middle finger.
This little mouse took a bite of cheese;	Bend down ring finger.
This little mouse heard a kitten sneeze;	Bend down pinkie finger.
"Ah-Choo!" sneezed the kitten, and "Squeak," they cried, As they found a hole and hid inside.	Put hand on hip and hide closed fist under arm.

Cats and mice are the main characters of many children's stories. As you read some of these books, encourage children to predict what they think the story will be about. The selections below include only those titles that include both cats and mice in the text. Read these aloud to the class.

Archambault, John and Bill Martin, Jr. *A Beautiful Feast for a Big King Cat.* HarperCollins, 1994.

Dubanevich, Arlene. *Tom's Tail.* Viking, 1990.

Geraghty, Paul. *Look Out, Patrick!* Macmillan, 1990.

Ginsburg, Mirra. *Three Kittens.* Crown, 1973.

Hoff, Syd. *Mrs. Brice's Mice.* HarperCollins, 1988.

Keats, Ezra Jack. *Kitten for a Day.* Macmillan, 1993.

Rayner, Shoo. *Cat in a Flap.* Puffin Books, 1992. (Lift-the-flap book)

Zelinsky, Paul O. *The Mail and the Mouse and the Odd-Shaped House.* Puffin, 1993.

1-2-3 RHYMES

1, 2, Buckle My Shoe

1, 2, 3, 4, Mary's at the Kitchen Door

Once I Caught a Fish Alive

This Old Man

1, 2, buckle my shoe.
3, 4, shut the door.
5, 6, pick up sticks.
7, 8, lay them straight.
9, 10, a big fat hen!

Introduce this rhyme by reading the must-have *Big Fat Hen* illustrated by Keith Baker (Harcourt Brace, 1994) to the class—a beautifully illustrated version of this verse.

Repeat this rhyme several times with children. Start in a whisper. On the last line say, "9, 10, begin again, a little bit louder." Say the rhyme a little louder each time until children are shouting! Stop with "9, 10, never again!"

🎲 Have children try saying the rhyme very slowly and then very fast. Have them recite it in very high voices and then in low voices. It's fun and great practice! They'll have it memorized in no time.

🎲 You will find a variation on the lines and motions to this popular nursery rhyme in Marc Brown's *Play Rhymes* (E. P. Dutton, 1987). Or you and the children can make up your own motions. Always pop up the appropriate number of fingers as children say each of the numbers.

🎲 Make cards to represent each object in the rhyme—a shoe, a door, sticks laying around, sticks in a neat row, and a hen—with your own simple line drawings or the ones on pages 268–272. Use these cards as clues when you say the rhyme with children. Then have five children each hold a card at the front of the room and stand as his or her line is said.

🎲 Write the rhyme on chart paper and laminate. Point to the words as you read the rhyme with children. Invite individuals to come to the chart and circle numbers, words, and other phonics and language conventions with a washable marker. For example, you might ask them to circle a specific numeral, circle the word that rhymes with each number, circle the commas, or underline the capital letters.

🎲 Count the number of words in each line and then in the whole rhyme (26 if you include the numerals and 16 if you don't). Which line has the most words?

Write each line of the rhyme on a sentence strip. Children can match the sentence strips to lines on the laminated chart paper. Have individual or small groups of children put the sentence strips in the correct order. Or choose five students to sit in a line in front of the class with a sentence strip. Children stand as their lines are read.

After children have mastered the rhyme using sentence strips, add number cards—one for each number 1 to 10. Have the appropriate children stand for each part of the rhyme. For example, for "1, 2, buckle my shoe," three children would stand—the child with the 1, the child with the 2, and the child with the shoe.

Cut all the sentence strips into individual words (only the words, not the numbers). Make a number graph by writing the numbers 1 through 10 across the bottom of a chalkboard. Put double-sided tape on the back of each word card. With children, count the number of letters in each word and stick each word card above the number that represents its letter total. Discuss the graph. Which number has the most words over it? the fewest? no words? Keep the graph up and add the words for each of the four rhymes in this unit.

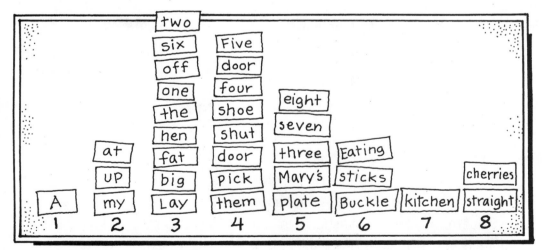

Ask volunteers to illustrate each line of the nursery rhyme. Put the illustrations in order and bind them together for a class book. Turn the pages of the illustrated book for picture cues when children say the rhyme together.

123 "1, 2, buckle my shoe." Collect small plastic doll shoes to use as counters (most parents of daughters have plenty of little shoes that don't match). Give each child an empty egg carton or muffin tin with numbers written with permanent marker in the bottom of each section. Children count the correct number of shoes into each section.

123 "5, 6, pick up sticks. 7, 8, lay them straight." Buy a set of small plastic colored plates and write a number in the center of each with permanent marker. Have each child "pick up" the appropriate number of toothpicks or craft sticks and put them on each plate. As children choose this game, ask them which line of the rhyme it represents.

123 "9, 10, a big fat hen!" Show children pictures of the colorful hens from Keith Baker's *Big Fat Hen*. Then have each child draw a simple outline of a fat hen. Get some feather dusters and have children cut individual feathers to add to their big fat hens.

123 Give out sticks from your rhythm-band instruments. Have children beat the sticks to a steady beat while others recite the rhyme.

123 Make "sticks and stones" by mixing stick pretzels and raisins. Have each child put a handful into a plastic zipper bag for snack. Before eating, challenge children to make the numbers 1 through 10 or their names using the sticks and the stones!

123 Use the rhyme to play a ball game. Have children choose partners and give each pair a playground ball. As the class recites the rhyme, the children with the balls bounce them to their partners on the numbers. The partners hold the balls on the words (younger children can roll the ball or throw a bean bag back and forth). Children continue back and forth—bouncing on the numbers and holding on the words as they say the rhyme.

More mature students may enjoy learning these additional lines to the rhyme, which are illustrated in many book versions.

> 11, 12, dig and delve.
>
> 13, 14, maids are courting.
>
> 15, 16, maids in the kitchen.
>
> 17, 18, maids are waiting.
>
> 19, 20, my plate is empty.

Once children have memorized the original verse, they are sure to enjoy the humor of Shel Silverstein's poem "One Two" from *A Light in the Attic* (HarperCollins, 1981). First, read it to the class with great expression! Then invite children to participate in an oral reading of the poem. Have them recite the lines that are the original Mother Goose verse and you read the lines that are the responses. Then change places and have the children say the responses with lots of expression. You might even encourage them to create their own responses to the Mother Goose lines!

For more rhyming practice (and more fun), consider helping children rewrite the story portions of the nursery rhyme. For example,

> One, two, find a canoe.
>
> Three, four, sit on the floor.
>
> Five, six, watch out for ticks!
>
> Seven, eight, that's too much weight!
>
> Nine, ten, we tipped over again!

Read Liz Underhill's *1, 2, Tie Up My Shoe: A New Look at an Old Rhyme* (Stewart, Tabori & Chang, 1990) an innovation of the traditional rhyme ("1, 2, tie up my shoe. 3, 4, away we roar . . .") with numbers to 30. After reading this rhyme to the class, encourage students to write their own innovations.

Share *One, Two Buckle My Shoe: A Book of Counting Rhymes* by Rowan Barnes-Murphy (Little Simon, 1987). This book includes many other counting rhymes that children will enjoy.

1, 2, 3, 4,
Mary's at the kitchen door,
5, 6, 7, 8,
Eating cherries off a plate.

Repeat this rhyme using the name of each child in the class (1, 2, 3, 4, *Amanda's* at the kitchen door . . .). Children love hearing their own names!

Hi-Ho! Cherry-O! is a game for ages 3–6 from Western Publishing Co. Each child gets ten plastic cherries on a tree. The children take turns spinning 1, 2, 3, or 4 to see how many cherries to take off the tree. The child who takes off all his or her cherries first wins. This is a great game for an adult or older child to teach to children in small groups. It is available in most toy stores or can be ordered from Creative Playthings, 1227 E. 119th St., Grandview, Missouri 64030-1117, 1-800-255-6124. The product number is Hi-Ho! Cherry-O! #WP-4703.

Write the rhyme on chart paper and laminate. Write numerals 1 through 8 on sticky notes and encourage children to match the numerals to the number words. If this is a new skill, children may need a chart to refer to (1 one, 2 two, and so on).

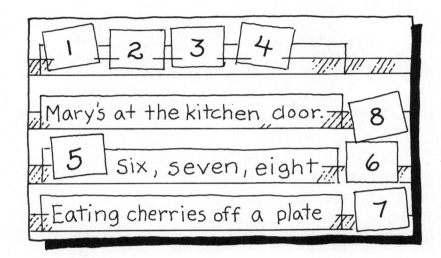

With children, count the number of lines in this verse. Count the number of words in each line. Count the number of words in the entire rhyme. Which line has the most words? the least? Which word has the most letters? Which word has the fewest letters?

Have children illustrate the rhyme with themselves instead of Mary in the picture, eating their favorite foods. "1, 2, 3, 4, (child's name) at the kitchen door. 5, 6, 7, 8, eating (food) off a plate." Write the rhyme for each child (more mature students can write it themselves) at the bottom of a clean sheet of white drawing paper, and have the child fill in the blanks. Display on a bulletin board.

Have each child make sticky notes with his or her name and favorite food. Have children take turns putting their sticky notes over the words on the laminated chart rhyme. Encourage the class to read each new rhyme.

Have children write innovations for this rhyme. Brainstorm a list of words that rhyme with *four* and *eight*. Then have children replace the second and last lines. Illustrate each new rhyme. For example,

1, 2, 3, 4,

Doggie wants a little more.

5, 6, 7, 8,

Guess that he'll just have to wait.

Bring in fresh cherries for children to taste or look for jars of red maraschino cherries. Encourage each child to taste a cherry, and then make a "Do you like cherries?" graph. Write *yes* on the left side and *no* on the right side. Give each child a clothespin to attach to the side that represents his or her response. Discuss the graph.

Do you like cherries?

Buy a set of colored plastic plates or bowls. Write a number on each one with permanent marker. Children can count the appropriate number of "cherries" into each bowl. For cherry counters, use red wooden beads from your bead-stringing set, red plastic or wooden beads from a craft store, red pompoms, or red plastic bingo chips.

The music for "Rickety Tickety" can be found in *Wee Sing Children's Songs and Fingerplays*. Put red dots on the inside tips of each child's fingers with a marker (this is optional).

Rickety tickety, look at me.

How many cherries do you see?

Hold up from one to ten fingers. Children say the appropriate number, perhaps three, and then everyone counts one, two, three. Repeat again with another number.

For each child, fold a piece of paper into eight sections. Children write or trace the numerals 1 through 8—one in each section. Then they use a red bingo dabber (available in the game section of most drug and department stores) to dab the appropriate number of "cherries" in each section. (You may also use corks, or fingertips dipped in red tempera paint or touched to a red washable ink pad).

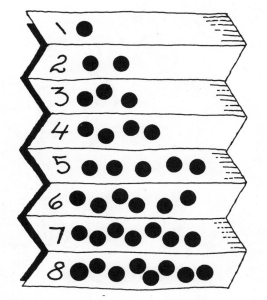

Put red paint at the easel this week and encourage children to make red cherries (circles). Or for something different, paint with cherry-flavored gelatin! Add water to dry gelatin and stir until it is the consistency of tempera paint or just add dry cherry gelatin to red tempera paint. The paint will have lumps but it will smell terrific! Have children paint on a flat surface to keep the paint from dripping.

Buy a box of Berry Berry Kix cereal from General Mills, which has yellow, red, and purple pieces, or Captain Crunch's Crunch Berries, which has only yellow corn cereal and red cherry-flavored pieces, for snack. Have each child pull out a large handful of cereal. As children put their hands into the box, repeat the rhyme with their names inserted. For example, "1, 2, 3, 4, Courtney's at the kitchen door. . . ." Then have children sort their cereal, putting like kinds together. Have children count first the purple and then the red (likely to be less than eight.) Decide with children which color group is most numerous (yellow).

Make a tasting graph. Have children taste each color of cereal and decide which they prefer. Draw the three types (a yellow circle, a red circle, and a purple circle) down the left side of a piece of construction paper. Invite each child to place one piece of his or her favorite color next to the appropriate picture and discuss the results. Which kind did we like the most? the least? More mature students may want to count the number in each row. Don't forget to let them eat their cereal!

1, 2, 3, 4, 5,
Once I caught a fish alive.
6, 7, 8, 9, 10,
Then I let him go again.

Why did you let him go?
Because he bit my finger so.
Which finger did he bite?
This little finger on the right.

Practice chanting this rhyme with children. After chanting is mastered, have them use motions to keep a steady beat—clapping, snapping fingers, hitting thighs, and so on.

Repeat the rhyme using the following motions.

1, 2, 3, 4, 5,	Pop up one finger at a time on one hand.
Once I caught a fish alive.	Pretend to reel in a fish.
6, 7, 8, 9, 10,	Pop up one finger at a time on other hand.
Then I let him go again.	Pretend to throw fish back in water.
Why did you let him go?	Put palms up by shoulders, questioning.
Because he bit my finger so.	Shake right hand.
Which finger did he bite?	Hold right hand still, palm up and open.
This little finger on the right.	Hold up pinky finger.

 With children count the number of lines in each verse. Count the number of words in each line. Count the number of words in each verse. Count the number of words in the entire rhyme! Which verse has the most words? the fewest? Which line has the most words? the fewest? Which word has the most letters? Which word has the fewest?

 Cut ten fish shapes from felt of different colors for your flannel board. As you say the rhyme, put up a fish for each number, one through ten. Leave the fish out for children to manipulate. Use the felt fish to practice identifying colors as well.

 Invite children to use stencils or crayons (try glitter crayons!) to draw ten fish of various sizes on pieces of white construction paper. Avoid blue crayons. Encourage children to fill all the white space inside their fish shapes with crayon. Then use crayon resist and have children paint over the entire page with a thin coat of blue tempera paint. When the paint is dry, give children gummed hole reinforcements to place above each fish's mouth to look like bubbles.

🎲 Have each child cut a fishbowl shape from white construction paper (or precut the shapes). Put five to ten drops of blue food coloring and a couple of drops of liquid dishwashing detergent into a cup. Fill the cup 1/3 full of water. Put each cup of water on a cookie sheet to catch the overflow. Place a straw into each cup and invite children to blow bubbles (the bubbles will soon overflow the cup). Children then stop and press their fishbowl shapes over the bubbles to make bubble prints. Then they blow some more and make another print on the same fishbowl shape—continuing until the bowl shape is covered with bubble prints. Let dry. Add small colored fish shapes cut from construction paper or use sponge fish shapes for sponge-painting fish. Display the fish pictures with a copy of the rhyme.

🎲 Enjoy pretzel fish for snack. Ask children how many they want and have them count the number that they asked for (or let each child roll a pair of game cubes and count out the number of fish they rolled). Practice subtraction by saying, "Eat (one, two, three). How many do you have left?"

🎲 Make edible miniaquariums. Give each child a rectangular cracker (saltine, whole graham cracker). Mix blue food coloring and whipped cream cheese to represent water. Give each child a plastic knife or tongue depressor to spread the blue cream cheese on the cracker. Have children predict how many fish crackers will fit in their "aquariums" and then test their predictions.

🎲 Give each child an empty egg carton with numbers written in the bottom of each section with permanent marker. Ask children to place the correct number of fish-shaped crackers into each section. Have an adult check to make sure the child has counted correctly, then invite children to eat their treats. Try this counting task each day for a week at snack time! Save the cartons to use for other counting activities.

🎲 Look for fish-shaped cookie cutters to add to your play dough area this week. Draw goldfish bowls directly on a plastic-laminate table top with permanent marker (hair spray or alcohol will remove the marker). Each day, write a different numeral in each bowl. Encourage children to make the appropriate number of fish for each bowl from play dough.

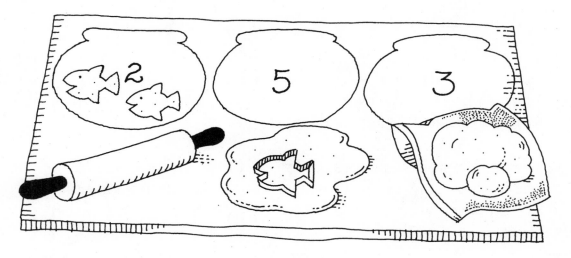

🎲 Make fish-shaped counting cards. Cut fish shapes from construction paper or use fish-shaped note pads. Write the numerals 1 to 10 on each fish. Laminate for durability. Show children the cards in order and randomly, and invite students to name each numeral you show. Leave the cards out so that children can practice sequencing them. Make other flashcard sets for identifying alphabet letters, number words, color words, and sight words.

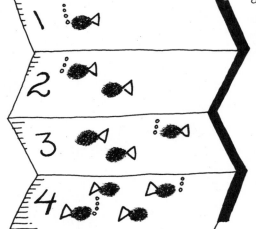

123 Write numbers down the left side of a sheet of paper for each child. Invite children to dip their index fingers in paint or press them on a washable ink pad to make the appropriate number of prints beside each number. Suggest that children turn each print into a fish by adding eyes and triangular tails.

123 Write the numbers 1 to 10 on the outsides of clear plastic cups with permanent marker—one number per cup. Place fish stickers on the outside of each cup. Invite children to place the corresponding number of "fish bubbles" (blue plastic bingo chips) inside each cup.

123 Float fish-shaped sponges (or fish cut from fun foam, available with craft supplies) in the water table. Invite children to use aquarium nets to catch some fish and then count the number of fish in their nets.

123 Play fish bingo. Cut a construction-paper fish shape for each child. Write four to eight numbers from 1 to 10 or from 1 to 20 on each fish in random order. Be sure the numbers are not too close together. Laminate the fish bingo cards for durability. Give each child a fish card and some fish-cracker markers or blue bingo-chip "bubbles." Cut 20 small fish from construction paper and write a number on each. Place these numbered fish in a bag (or fish bowl) and mix them up. Draw out one fish and call out the number on it. Children who have that number on their cards cover it with a marker. Continue drawing cards and calling numbers until one child has all his or her numbers covered. Instead of number bingo, you might also try number word bingo, alphabet bingo, shape bingo, color-word bingo, and sight-word bingo.

 Have an adult volunteer teach children to play go fish. Select all the numbered cards from a deck of cards. Deal seven cards to each child if there are two players and five cards to each child if there are three or four players. Place the rest of the cards face down in the "fish pond" in the center of the playing space. The object of the game is to match number pairs. Each player, in turn, asks another player to give him or her all of the cards with a specified number. For example, a player may say to another child, "Give me all your threes." If the child asked does not have any threes, he or she responds, "Go fish!" The first child then draws a card from the fish pond and play passes to the next child. Players place their matching pairs of cards face up in front of them. When the pond is empty, the child with the most matching pairs wins.

 Put ten numbered fish in sequence at the front of the room. Have a child come to the front while the rest of the children have their eyes closed and turn one fish over. Have the class guess which number is missing. The child who guesses correctly gets to have the next turn. For more challenge, place the fish in random sequence.

Share these fish counting and number books with children.

Dr. Seuss. *One Fish Two Fish Red Fish Blue Fish.* Random House, 1987.

Edwards, Roberta. *Five Silly Fishermen.* Random House, 1989.

Ehlert, Lois. *Fish Eyes: A Book You Can Count On.* Harcourt Brace Jovanovich, 1990.

McCarthy, Patricia. *Ocean Parade: A Counting Book.* Dial Books, 1990.

Wise, William. *Ten Sly Piranhas: A Counting Story in Reverse.* Dial, 1993.

Enjoy this traditional fingerplay while teaching ordinal numbers.

Five little fishes swimming in the pool.   Pretend to swim.

The first one said, "This pool is cool."   Pop up little finger.

The second one said, "This pool is deep."   Pop up ring finger.

The third one said, "I'd like to sleep."   Pop up middle finger and pretend to sleep.

The fourth one said,
   "Let's swim and dip."   Pop up index finger.

The fifth one said, "I see a ship."   Pop out thumb.

The fisherman's line went
   splish, splash, splash   Pretend to throw line into water.

And away the five little fish did dash!   Quickly hide hand behind back.

This old man, he played one, he played nick nack on my thumb. (Refrain)

This old man, he played two, he played nick nack on my shoe. (Refrain)

This old man, he played three, he played nick nack on my knee. (Refrain)

This old man, he played four, he played nick nack on my door. (Refrain)

This old man, he played five, he played nick nack on my hive. (Refrain)

This old man, he played six, he played nick nack on some sticks. (Refrain)

This old man, he played seven, he played nick nack up to heaven. (Refrain)

This old man, he played eight, he played nick nack on my gate. (Refrain)

This old man, he played nine, he played nick nack on a line. (Refrain)

This old man, he played ten, he played nick nack with a hen. (Refrain)

(Refrain)

With a nick nack paddywack give the dog a bone,

This old man came rolling home!

A traditional tune for this nursery rhyme can be found in Pamela Beall and Susan Nipp's *Wee Sing Nursery Rhymes and Lullabies* (Price, Stern & Sloan, 1985). The *Wee Sing* set comes with an audio cassette and sing-along book. It is easily found in most toy, book, or school-supply stores or can be ordered directly from Price, Stern & Sloan Publishers, Inc., 410 North La Cienega Boulevard, Los Angeles, CA 90048. This version includes motions for all ten verses and for the the refrain.

Tony Ross's *This Old Man: A Musical Counting Book* (Aladdin Books, 1990) is a wonderful introduction to this rhyme. It has clear, fun illustrations for the verses one to ten and includes a music chip, so children can hear and sing the words. Or enjoy Robin Michael Koontz's *This Old Man: The Counting Rhyme* (Dodd, Mead, 1988), which illustrates the rhyme to ten. This version has suggestions for actions, the tune, and some history about the origin of the rhyme. Carol Jones's *This Old Man* (Houghton Mifflin, 1995) illustrates the rhyme with circles die-cut into each page. Inside the circle is each number's rhyming word. Another adorable rendition of this old favorite is Pam Adams' oversized *This Old Man* (Child's Play, 1996) with die-cut holes and fun illustrations for verses one to six.

Here is one version of motions to use when singing the refrain.

With a nick nack paddywack	Hit fists together top to bottom twice on *nick nack* and clap twice on *paddywack*.
Give the dog a bone,	Pretend to throw the dog a bone.
This old man came rolling home!	Roll hands over one another.

1 2 3   *Nick nack paddywack* are fun nonsense words. Enjoy the spirit of the words by having children substitute a different initial consonant for those words and then complete the rhyme. For example, *Bick, back, baddywack, give the dog a bone. This old man came rolling home.* Try going straight through the alphabet, singing a verse for each letter (eliminate the vowels, *c*, *x*, and *y*) or have children call out letters to try.

1 2 3   Make picture cards for this rhyme by making simple line drawings or by photocopying and coloring the pictures on pages 268–272. The cards will give children visual clues. Invite ten children to stand up in front of the class, with each child holding one picture card and children standing in order. Children hold up their cards at the appropriate times as the class sings or says the rhyme.

1 2 3   Write the verses on chart paper, using picture symbols for some of the words and numerals (see pages 268–272). Laminate the chart. Point to each word as you "read" the rhyme with the class. Match the pictures to words. When you come to a picture or number, stop so that children say the appropriate word on their own.

1 2 3   Each day, have children use a washable marker on the chart in the above activity to mark concepts that you wish to teach. For example, children might circle rhyming pairs, circle specific numbers, underline capital letters, or circle commas.

1 2 3   Count the number of words in each line. Which line has the most words? the fewest? Count the number of words in the refrain. Which word has the most letters? Which word has the fewest letters? Count the number of *n*'s in the rhyme. Count the capital letters. The possibilities are endless.

1 2 3   Make a class reproduction of the verses of this popular song on ten large sheets of paper. Write a pair of lines along the bottom of each sheet and illustrate as indicated on the following page.

This old man he played one,
He played nick nack on my thumb.

> thumbprint of each child

two • shoe

> Trace around each child's shoe.

three • knee

> Put water-based paint on each child's knee and print.

four • door

> Draw a door and add a button doorknob or take an instant photo of a door.

five • hive

> Draw a hive and have each child make a bumblebee.

six • sticks

> Collect small sticks and dip them into different colors of paint. Each child chooses a stick and uses it like a pencil to make lines and shapes.

seven • heaven

> Sponge-paint with white and light blue paint, then have each child add star or angel stickers to the "heavens."

eight • gate

> Use craft sticks dipped in brown paint to print a gate. Add details with markers.

nine • spine

> Paint a spine with white paint on black paper.

ten • hen

> Have each child draw a hen on the page.

🎲 After making the reproduction with the class (see previous activity), photocopy the words of each number couplet on individual pages to make a booklet for each child. Encourage children to illustrate their own versions.

🎲 Point out the rhyming word for each number. Then have children brainstorm a list of rhyming words for each number. Point out that all of the rhymes are not perfect (for example, *thumb* and *one*). After children have created rhyme lists, encourage them to write their own couplets for each number and illustrate each one. For example,

> This old man, he played one.
>
> He was silly and he had fun!
>
> This old man, he played two.
>
> He was scary and he said, "Boo!"
>
> This old man, he played three.
>
> He was running from a bee!

🎲 "... give the dog a bone." Buy a box of bone-shaped dog biscuits and spray them with high-gloss varnish or acrylic so you can use them as counters. (Bones do not *have* to be sprayed for this activity, but it will help to keep them from breaking as children manipulate them.) Cut some dog shapes from construction paper or tagboard and laminate. Write a number on each dog. Children can count out the appropriate number of bones for each dog.

🎲 Bury the bones from the previous activity in the sand table and have children count the bones as they find them.

🎲 Teach children the game doggie, doggie, who's got the bone. Use a rawhide dog bone for the game. Children sit in a circle or at their desks. One child is chosen to come to the middle (or front) and covers his or her eyes (or sits with his or her back to the group) with the bone in front of him or her. Another child quietly comes up, picks up the bone, and sings in a well-disguised voice, "Nick nack paddywack, give the dog a bone," then returns to his or her place. The chosen child tries to guess who has the bone. If the guess is incorrect, the child with the bone gets to be the chosen one. If the guess is correct, the first child gets another turn. The object is to be the guesser for as long as possible.

🎲 Children will enjoy this nursery rhyme about another dog and bone.

Old Mother Hubbard

Went to the cupboard

To fetch her poor dog a bone.

But when she got there

The cupboard was bare,

And so the poor dog had none.

Share with children the following books based on the rhyme.

Kessler, Leonard. *The Silly Mother Hubbard.* Garrard, 1980.

Martin, Sarah Catherine. *Old Mother Hubbard and Her Dog.* Holt, Rinehart & Winston, 1972.

O'Brien, John. *Mother Hubbard's Christmas.* Boyds Nills Press, 1996.

Provensen, Alice and Martin. *Old Mother Hubbard.* Random House Books for Young Readers, 1992.

Rader, Laura. *Mother Hubbard's Cupboard: A Mother Goose Surprise Book.* Tambourine Books, 1993.

Counting Activities

Make an audio tape for your listening center. Include counting rhymes chanted and sung by the class as well as commercial recordings. Also include the class and individual students counting from 1 to 10 or from 1 to 20 throughout the tape.

Rote count every day using fingers. First, master 1, 2, 3, 4, 5, 6, 7, 8, 9, 10. Have children pop up a finger for each number. Have children shout the number 10, flashing the 10 by opening and closing their fists. After children have mastered counting to 10, count to 20. Make fists after 10 and pop up fingers again, 1 finger for 11, 2 for 12, 3 for 13, and so on, shouting and flashing on 20.

Count s-l-o-w-ly. Count fast. Whisper-count, ending with fingers to lips, "Shhhh." Count LOUDLY!

Count scary! For scary numbers, say each number using fingers, wiggling your voice like you'd say "Who-o-o" for a ghost at Halloween. End with a loud, "Boo!"

Count mad! For mad numbers, count with a mad face hitting fists alternately on the floor.

Count sad! For crying numbers, count with a sad face while pretending to cry.

Count happy! For happy numbers, count with a happy face and sing-song voice.

Anything to make counting fun and interesting!

Make up motions as you count, such as clapping hands to 10 and hitting thighs to 20, or any other motions that children enjoy. Each day, choose a different child to come up and lead the counting.

123 Count to morning exercises. Have each child lead an excercise, such as touching toes or swinging arms side-to-side. Count as you exercise.

123 Have each child make a number book. Give each child a ten-page blank booklet. Have children cut the numbers 1 to 10 from magazines and glue one number on each page. Children then draw sets of objects; stick on gummed dots, stars, or stickers; or use a rubber stamp or bingo dabber to represent each number.

123 There are many counting books appropriate for this age group. Here are some favorites, but do not limit yourself to this list. Ask your librarian for suggestions.

Anno, Mitsumasa. *Anno's Counting Book.* HarperCollins, 1977.

Baker, Alan. *Gray Rabbit's 1,2,3.* Kingfisher Books, 1994.

Bang, Molly. *Ten, Nine, Eight.* Greenwillow, 1983.

Bond, Michael. *Paddington's 123.* Puffin, 1990.

Carlstrom, Nancy White. *Let's Count It Out, Jesse Bear.* Simon & Schuster, 1996.

Carter, David. *How Many Bugs in a Box?* Little Simon, 1988.

Crews, Donald. *Ten Black Dots.* Greenwillow, 1986.

Falwell, Cathryn. *Feast for 10.* Clarion, 1993.

Freschet, Bernice and Stephan Martin. *The Ants Go Marching.* Scribner, 1975.

Inkpen, Mick. *Kipper's Book of Numbers.* Red Wagon Books, 1994.

Martin, Bill, Jr. *Ten Little Caterpillars.* Holt, 1967.

Pallotta, Jerry. *The Icky Bug Counting Book.* The Trumpet Club, 1992.

Shade, Susan and Jon Buller. *Hello! Hello! A Counting Book.* Simon & Schuster, 1991.

Sturges, Philemon. *Ten Flashing Fireflies.* North-South Books, 1995.

Walsh, Ellen Stoll. *Mouse Count.* Voyager, 1991.

SPLISH SPLASH RHYMES

Jack and Jill
Rub~a~dub~dub
Rain, Rain, Go Away
It's Raining, It's Pouring
Itsy Bitsy Spider

Jack and Jill went up the hill
To fetch a pail of water;
Jack fell down and broke his crown,
And Jill came tumbling after.

A traditional tune for this nursery rhyme can be found in Pamela Beall and Susan Nipp's *Wee Sing Nursery Rhymes and Lullabies* (Price, Stern & Sloan, 1985). The *Wee Sing* set comes with an audio cassette and sing-along book. It is easily found in most toy, book, or school-supply stores or can be ordered directly from Price, Stern & Sloan Publishers, Inc., 410 North La Cienega Boulevard, Los Angeles, CA 90048.

Look for the board book *Jack and Jill: A Look Again Book* by Eleanor Wasmuth (Little Simon, 1986) as an introduction to this rhyme. This simple book illustrates the rhyme line by line.

 Have children sing the rhyme very s-l-o-w-ly and then very fast. Have them sing the song in a very high "Jill" voice and then in a low "Jack" voice. Sing the rhyme once very loudly and then whisper it softly. Go around the room and ask each child to choose a way for the class to sing the rhyme.

 Invite children to chant this rhyme as they clap a steady beat. After children master clapping the beat, have them think of other movements. Select children to lead a motion, such as swaying side-to-side, tapping index fingers, touching toes and then putting hands on waist, or hitting hands to thighs. Bring out the rhythm instruments and have children use triangles to keep the beat. Do triangles sound like raindrops on the roof?

Children love to act out this rhyme. Use the steps on the bottom of a rocking boat or two chairs at either end of a low table for the hill. A large trash can makes a great well. The children (a boy and a girl) carry a sand pail up the hill to the well and then take turns walking down the hill. Each child somersaults or falls down as Jack breaks his crown and Jill comes tumbling after. Use children's real names (Johnny and Maree went up the hill . . .). Have different pairs take turns acting the parts while the class recites the rhyme. Be prepared to do this over and over and over.

This is a perfect rhyme to sequence. Choose the three major events: 1) Jack and Jill walk up the hill with the pail; 2) Jack falls down; 3) Jill falls down. Draw stick figures on index cards to represent each event, find illustrations in an old nursery rhyme book to cut out and laminate, or trace some appealing illustrations. After you have discussed the sequence with the class, photocopy the pictures on one page and make a copy for each child. Have children cut out and practice sequencing the events. Encourage children to take their sequence cards home to show their families as they practice the rhyme.

Have children recite the rhyme with the following motions.

Jack and Jill went up the hill to fetch a pail of water;	Sit on floor, legs crossed, and pretend to climb hill by placing one hand over the other continuously until hands are over head.
Jack fell down	Hit right thigh with right hand.
and broke his crown,	Hit left thigh with left hand.
And Jill came tumbling after.	Roll hands one over the other.

 With the children, brainstorm a list of words that rhyme with *Jill* and *hill* (*ill, drill, chill, shrill,* and so on). Use the list to create rhyming couplets using the first line of the rhyme. For example,

Jack and Jill went up the hill

So that they could play with Bill.

Jack and Jill went up the hill.

For all I know they're up there still!

 Have children identify the opposites *up* and *down* in the rhyme. Then have each child think of a pair of opposites or brainstorm a list of opposites with the class. Invite each child to choose a pair of opposites, such as *boy* and *girl* or *open* and *closed*. Give each child a sheet of drawing paper divided in half. Write one opposite word on each half of the paper and invite children to illustrate their words. Bind the drawings together to make a class book of opposites.

Write the rhyme on chart paper and laminate. Each day, have students come up and use a washable marker to practice identifying language and phonics skills. For example, they might make an X where you start to read, underline all the words with a capital *J,* circle a word that rhymes with *hill,* circle words with the short *i* sound, or underline a word that rhymes with *down.*

Discuss the vocabulary in this rhyme. Can children find a picture of a well in one of your nursery-rhyme collection books? What does *fetch* mean? (get) Can you think of another nursery rhyme that uses the word *fetch?* (Old Mother Hubbard) What is Jack's *crown?* (head, where a crown would fit) Think of other nursery rhymes that have crowns ("Old King Cole," "Sing a Song of Sixpence," "The Queen of Hearts").

Write the lines of the rhyme on sentence strips. Draw or use the pictures on pages 268–272 for some of the key words (*Jack, Jill, hill, pail, water*). As you read the rhyme with the class, stop at the pictures and have children say the appropriate words. Write the words on sticky notes and encourage students to come up to the chart and put the words over the appropriate pictures.

Most nursery-rhyme collections include this rhyme. Enjoy collections that include additional verses for this favorite nursery rhyme, such as the extended "Jack and Jill" in Tomie DePaola's *Hey Diddle Diddle and Other Mother Goose Rhymes* (G. P. Putnam's Sons, 1988).

Have children choose a friend and illustrate the following lines of the poem, filling in the names of themselves and a friend. Children can even change the pail of water to something else they would like to fetch. "*Courtney* and *Amanda* went up a hill to fetch *a pan of brownies*." Have children illustrate their new sentences. Display them on a bulletin board with the title, "Jack and Jill Went Up a Hill . . ." After children have enjoyed the display, bind the pictures into a class book.

 Brainstorm a list of reasons why Jack and Jill went up the hill for water. What happened after they fell down? Then encourage students to write and illustrate their own Jack and Jill adventures.

 "*Up* the hill" and "Jack fell *down* . . ." As you discuss the concepts *up* and *down* with children, teach them the popular rhyme "Ring Around the Rosie" with children holding hands in a circle.

> Ring around the rosie.
>
> A pocket full of posies.
>
> Ashes, ashes.
>
> We all fall down!

And all the children fall down and dissolve in giggles! Other *up*-and-*down* songs that children will enjoy are "The Noble Duke of York" and "London Bridge Is Falling Down."

Look for adaptations of this rhyme such as the one found in Diane Loomans' *Positively Mother Goose*. Have children think up other happy endings to the rhyme.

On a bulletin board or wall, enlarge a picture of the well from one of the Jack and Jill rhymes and add the title "Wishing Well Words." Place word cards from these rhymes all around the well as you do this unit. Write each word on a sentence strip and have volunteers illustrate the words on index cards. Glue the index card to the end of the sentence strip (which can be cut in half). Or find rhyming pairs and put them on sand-pail shapes all around the well. Play games with the words, such as "Find a word with three letters." "Find a word that rhymes with _____." "Find a word from the Jack and Jill rhyme." "Find a word with a capital letter." "Find a word that means _____."

Wishing Well Words

Make a Jack and Jill graph. Have each child draw a self-portrait or take an instant photo of each child. For the graph, draw a picture of Jack and a picture of Jill. All the girls put their pictures over Jill and all the boys put their pictures over Jack. Make sure to include yourself. Count the number of Jacks and the number of Jills. Discuss this simple graph—are there more girls or more boys? How many more?

J is a popular letter for proper names. Have children brainstorm a list of girls' and boys' names that begin with *J*. If you have a name-the-baby book, bring it in so children can find other names. Leave the list up and encourage children to add to it as the week goes along. If children enjoy this game, have each child make a list of names that begin with the same letter as his or her name.

Add some sand pails of different sizes to your water table and measuring cups or other paper and plastic cups. Challenge children to discover how many cups it takes to fill a pail. Before filling the pail, have children estimate how many cups they think it will take. Then they actually count as they fill, comparing their guesses to the resulting number of cups.

Children will enjoy finding Jack and Jill in Janet and Allan Ahlberg's *Each Peach Pear Plum* (Puffin Books, 1989). This is a great book to read to a child in your lap or to send home for parents to read to their children.

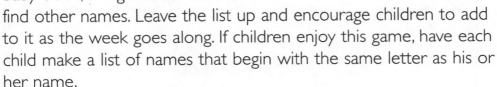

Rub-a-dub-dub,
Three men in a tub,
And who do you think they be?
The butcher, the baker, the candlestick maker,
And all of them gone to sea.

Review the vocabulary in this rhyme. Find a picture of the rhyme (or photocopy the one above) and mount on a large piece of tagboard. With the class, label the vocabulary in the picture (*tub, butcher, baker, candlestick maker, sea*). Talk about the jobs of each worker. Children will find other things to label that do not relate directly to the poem, which is fine. Go over the words that the class has identified each day, pointing out those that specifically relate to the rhyme.

A traditional tune for this nursery rhyme can be found in Pamela Beall and Susan Nipp's *Wee Sing Nursery Rhymes and Lullabies* (Price, Stern & Sloan, 1985). The *Wee Sing* set comes with an audio cassette and sing-along book. It is easily found in most toy, book, or school-supply stores or can be ordered directly from Price, Stern & Sloan Publishers, Inc., 410 North La Cienega Boulevard, Los Angeles, CA 90048.

Recite the rhyme using the cloze method. Say each line, stopping expectantly before the last word. Children fill in the word.

Act out the rhyme. For the butcher, use a plastic foam meat tray with a plastic lamb chop or rubber roast from your housekeeping center. You can also add a white apron cut from a white garbage bag. For the baker, use a chef's hat (a white band around the head with a large paper dinner napkin stapled to the band at the corners and tucked into the band); a white apron cut from a plastic garbage bag; and any baking prop, such as a rolling pin or plastic cake. For the candlestick maker, use a candle. Each worker holds his or her prop. As you say each worker's part, he or she climbs into a big box or your rocking boat. End the rhyme with a rousing verse of "Row, Row, Row Your Boat."

Ask children why a butcher, a baker, and a candlestick maker would go out to sea in a tub! Or ask them to think of some adventures the three might have on their voyage. Where would they go? What might they see? After your discussion, invite each child to draw one of the adventures and dictate a few sentences about it. More advanced students can write their own adventure stories about the three men at sea.

Since you have the candle out, teach children the popular

Jack be nimble, Jack be quick,

Jack jump over the candlestick!

Be sure to put out a candlestick and have all the children jump over it in turn, using each child's name in place of *Jack*.

Have parents collect used candles to send in. Don't forget used birthday candles and floating candles that come in neat shapes. Float the candles in your water table and encourage children to compare, sort, and order by length, thickness, color, and so on.

Use the drawings on pages 268–272, have children draw the characters, or cut appropriate pictures from old nursery rhyme books to make craft-stick puppets. You will need a butcher, a baker, a candlestick maker, and a tub—each on the end of a craft stick. Use these (and have children use) to illustrate the rhyme as the class recites it. Leave out the puppets for children to play with during choice times or have each child make a set to take home.

Change the rhyme to include the names of three children.

Rub-a-dub-dub,

Three kids in a tub,

And who do you think they be?

It's Robert and Ruthie and Rosie,

All of them gone, you see.

Act out the rhyme by having each child climb into a box or rocking boat when his or her name is called and then jump out and hide on the last line. Have the three children illustrate the rhyme by drawing or painting a picture of themselves with two of their friends in a tub, going to sea.

 Make a class mural. For the background, sponge-paint the sea in shades of blue. Then have children cut out large tub-boat shapes. Children draw self-portraits, cut around the pictures, and add themselves to the floating boats (or use instant photos of each child). Make sure to include yourself! Add the title, "Rub-a-dub-dub! Three Kids in a Tub!"

 You can also make a class book. On each light-blue page, add a dark blue sea and a brown tub cut from construction paper. Take instant photos of each child standing up. Trim the pictures and cover with wide clear tape to make them more durable. On the top of each page, write

> Rub-a-dub-dub
>
> Three kids in a tub!
>
> Who do you think they be?

At the bottom of the page, write

> All of them gone to sea!

The tub is in the middle. Children can put any three kids in the tub and read the page with the names of the children they chose. Some children will sit with this book for concentrated periods of time, changing all the pictures around and reading the rhyme over and over.

Write the entire rhyme on sentence strips. Have children watch you cut the sentence strips into individual words. Place these words in order in a pocket chart and read the rhyme with the class. Then have children close their eyes while one child comes up and turns one word over. Children open their eyes and try to guess the mystery word. The child who guesses correctly takes the next turn.

After you have cut the rhyme into individual words, give them out to students. Display the rhyme on chart paper and help children make each line of the rhyme by bringing up the words for one line and placing them in order in a pocket chart. Read the line together and then go to the next line.

Use the cut-apart words as sight-word flashcards or challenge groups or individual children to put the whole rhyme back together on the floor or in a pocket chart.

Help children brainstorm a list of words that rhyme with *rub*, *dub*, and *tub*, such as *scrub* and *cub*. Invite children to use two words on the list to create different endings to the rhyme. For example,

> Rub-a-dub-dub
>
> Three men in a tub.
>
> They pulled the plug
>
> And went blub, blub, blub!
>
> Rub-a-dub-dub
>
> Three men in a tub
>
> Got soap and a brush
>
> And had a scrub.

Rub-a-dub-dub, have fun in the tub! What's more fun than bubble bath in the tub! Pour bubble bath in your water table for lots of fun. Bring all the baby dolls to the water table for a rub-a-dub-dub bubble bath!

Play "rub-a-dub-dub." Have children sit in a circle and ask one to leave the room. Give a small bar of soap to one of the children in the circle. The child who left comes back in and has three guesses to figure out who has the soap. If he or she guesses correctly, the person who was holding the soap leaves and the guesser gets to give the soap to someone new.

 Children will enjoy another threesome that took to sea—in a shoe! Look for *Wynken, Blynken, & Nod* by Eugene Field (North-South Books, 1995). Compare and contrast the characters and the mode of transportation in a "Rub-a-dub-dub" with those in "Wynken, Blynken, and Nod."

Rain, rain, go away,
Come again another day.
Little children want to play.
Rain, rain, go away.

It's raining. It's pouring.
The old man is snoring.
Went to bed with a cold in his head
And didn't get up 'til morning.

Invest in some inexpensive rain slickers to keep children dry (or throw-away rain ponchos, raincoats used by patrols on rainy days, or heavy-duty garbage bags with holes cut for faces) and go for a walk in the rain! Sing the nursery rhymes as you go or sing your own rendition of "Raindrops Keep Falling on My Head" or "Singin' in the Rain."

 Say each line of these nursery rhymes and have children echo the lines back to you. Divide children into two groups. Have one group say a line and have the other group echo it.

 Chant the rhymes while children keep a steady beat by clapping, stamping feet, tapping toes, or nodding heads. Get out rhythm instruments and give each child one rhythm stick. Tap them on the floor to a steady beat and see if children think this sounds like rain.

 Have children sit in a circle with you. When you lift your arm up high, children shout the rhymes. When you hold your arm in the middle, children say the rhymes in a normal tone. When you have your hand on the floor, children whisper the rhymes. Move your hand up and down as children follow your lead with their voices. Then choose a child to be the leader.

 Go around the circle and substitute children's names in each of the rhymes.

> Rain, rain, go away.
>
> Kim and Shamika want to play.
>
> It's raining. It's pouring.
>
> Johnny is snoring.

(Be sure Johnny pretends to snore!)

Have children illustrate "It's raining. It's pouring." with themselves in the pictures. Pictures might include windows with rain on them and children asleep inside, getting their z-z-z-z's, or rainy outdoor scenes with kids in raincoats. Have each child draw his or her own interpretation.

On a day that you are sure it is going to rain, have each child choose a piece of white art paper to lay outside. Sprinkle different colors of dry tempera paint onto their papers. Invite children to watch from the windows as the rain falls and mixes the colors. Allow the pictures to dry indoors.

Introduce the following nursery rhyme to the class.

> Rain on the green grass.
> Rain on the tree.
> Rain on the housetop
> But not on me!

Encourage children to illustrate the poem. Brainstorm ideas before children begin to draw (children in raincoats; umbrellas; dancing in mud puddles; rain falling on trees, houses, and flowers). Look for an audio tape of spring rain sounds to play while children are drawing.

Look for other rain poetry to introduce to the class, such as "Dancin' in the Rain" from *Falling Up* by Shel Silverstein (HarperCollins, 1996) and "Rain" and "Lazy Jane" from *Where the Sidewalk Ends* by Shel Silverstein (HarperCollins, 1974). Encourage children to illustrate their favorite poems or write out one of these poems as a centerpiece for a bulletin-board display of the rain pictures done in the previous activity.

Teach children this traditional rhyme about thunder to the tune of "Frère Jacques."

I hear thunder. I hear thunder.	Sitting, drum hands on floor.
Listen now. Listen now.	Pretend to listen, hands cupped around ears.
Raindrops are falling. Raindrops are falling.	Pretend to make rain with fingers.
Pitter-patter-pat. Pitter-patter-pat.	Hit palms lightly on knees.

Children will also enjoy the delightful song, "If All the Raindrops Were Lemon Drops and Gumdrops," which is available in many song books for young children or with Barney music. It goes nicely with Judi Barrett's *Cloudy With a Chance of Meatballs* (Macmillan, 1978). Have children brainstorm the things they would like to see fall from the sky! Give children raindrop-shaped pieces of light-blue construction paper and have them finish the sentence, "It's raining (cats and dogs)!" with illustrations on their raindrops. Display on a bulletin board with a large, colorful umbrella.

Have each child finish the line *When it rains, (child's name) likes to* _____. Give each child a piece of drawing paper with this unfinished line written at the bottom. After completing the line, children illustrate what they like to do on rainy days. Display the illustrations or bind them together for a class book.

Children will enjoy all these books about rain, but do not limit yourself to these titles. Your librarian will be glad to make other suggestions. Keep some of these in a special box of rainy-day books that can be brought out and read only on rainy days.

Branley, Franklyn M. *Flash, Crash, Rumble and Roll*. Harper, 1985.

Carlstrom, Nancy. *What Does the Rain Play?* Macmillan, 1993.

Carlson, Nancy. *What If It Never Stops Raining?* Viking, 1992.

Ernst, Lisa Campbell. *Up to Ten and Down Again*. Lothrop, Lee & Shepard, 1986.

Ginsburg, Mirra. *Mushroom in the Rain*. Macmillan, 1990.

Greene, Carol. *Rain! Rain!* Childrens Press, 1982.

Hest, Amy. *In the Rain With Baby Duck*. Candlewick Press, 1995.

James, Betsy. *The Mud Family*. Putnam, 1994.

Johnson, Angela. *Rain Feet*. Orchard, 1994.

Kalan, Robert. *Rain*. Greenwillow Books, 1978.

Markle, Sandra. *A Rainy Day*. Orchard Books, 1992.

Martin, Bill, Jr., and John Archambault. *Listen to the Rain*. Henry Holt, 1988.

McCloskey, Robert. *Time of Wonder*. Penguin, 1957.

O'Brien, Anne Sibley. *Rainy City Rainbow*. Newbridge, 1996. (big book)

Rayner, Mary. *The Rain Cloud*. Atheneum, 1980.

Serfozo, Mary. *Rain Talk*. Margaret K. McElderry Books, 1990.

Shulevitz, Uri. *Rain Rain Rivers*. Farrar, Straus, & Giroux, 1969.

Spier, Peter. *Peter Spier's Rain*. Doubleday, 1982.

Tresselt, Alvin. *Rain Drop Splash*. Lothrop, 1946.

Tashima, Taro. *Umbrella in the Rain*. Puffin Books, 1986.

 Make it rain in your classroom! Place watering cans and sieves, bought or homemade, in your water table. You can make your own sieves by punching holes in the bottom of plastic or tin containers with a nail or push pin. Collect cottage cheese containers, yogurt cups, butter tubs, pie tins, pot pie tins, and so on. Poke different numbers and sizes of holes in the bottom of each container—large holes for "pouring" and smaller holes for "sprinkling." Raindrops keep falling on my head . . . oops! No heads, please!

 A favorite rain story of children of all ages is the story of Noah and the ark. Enjoy some of the following stories about Noah's ark and the 40 days and 40 nights of rain.

Anholt, Catherine. *Two by Two*. Candlewick Press, 1992.

Hawksley, Julie. *The Story of Noah's Ark*. Gallery Books, 1991.

Hayward, Linda. *Noah's Ark*. Random House, 1987.

Hewitt, Kathryn. *Two by Two: The Untold Story*. Harcourt Brace Jovanovich, 1984.

Ludwig, Warren. *Old Noah's Elephants*. Whitebird Books, 1991.

Serfozo, Mary. *Rain Talk*. Margaret K. McElderry Books, 1990.

Spier, Peter. *Noah's Ark*. Doubleday, 1985.

Write one numeral each on sheets of rainbow or umbrella note pads and laminate. Have children count the appropriate number of raindrops onto each number card. For raindrops, use blue plastic bingo chips or blue teardrop-shaped beads (available with craft supplies).

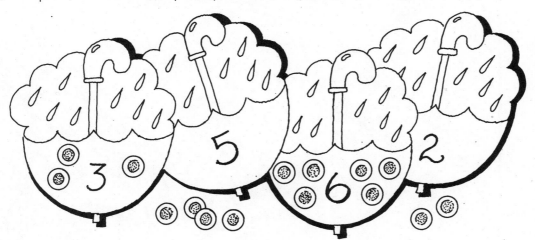

Look for appropriately shaped note pads to use as flashcards for numeral recognition, name recognition, uppercase and lowercase letter recognition, sight or Dolch words, spelling words, and so on. More mature students can supply words that start or end with a letter that you flash. Note pads appropriate for this unit include Noah's ark designs, umbrella and rain designs, and rainbow designs (from Frank Shaffer, Shapes Etc., and Carson-Dellosa). Look also for calendar numerals with a rain or April shower motif that can be used on calendars, sequenced individually, or used as flashcards with small groups.

Remind children that after the rain, there is usually a sparkling rainbow! Have children use watercolors to paint a rainbow with a bright sun. Display on the bulletin board with the title, "After the Rain. . . ."

Keep a special box of rainy-day books, reinforcing these rhymes on rainy days. Before you know it, children will be starting the rhymes each time it rains without your initiation.

The itsy, bitsy spider climbed up the waterspout.
Down came the rain and washed the spider out.
Out came the sun and dried up all the rain.
And the itsy, bitsy spider climbed up the spout again.

A traditional tune for this nursery rhyme can be found in Pamela Beall and Susan Nipp's *Wee Sing Nursery Rhymes and Lullabies* (Price, Stern & Sloan, 1985). The *Wee Sing* set comes with an audio cassette and sing-along book. It is easily found in most toy, book, or school-supply stores or can be ordered directly from Price, Stern & Sloan Publishers, Inc., 410 North La Cienega Boulevard, Los Angeles, CA 90048.

The Wright Group (1990) publishes this rhyme line-for-line in *The Eency Weency Spider*, illustrated by Alan Daniel. It comes in both big-book and paperback reader format as part of their "Song Box" series. This must-have introduction to this favorite song includes teacher ideas for using the books as well.

Sing or say the song with these traditional motions.

The itsy, bitsy spider Climbed up the water spout.	Touch thumb of one hand to index finger of other hand and switch back and forth as you raise arms.
Down came the rain	Arms overhead, wiggle fingers as you bring arms down.
And washed the spider out.	Hold straight arms directly in front and sweep arms out to sides.
Out came the sun	Arms form a circle overhead, index fingers touching, to make sun.
And dried up all the rain.	Wiggle fingers as arms go from low to high overhead. Lower arms.
And the itsy, bitsy spider Climbed up the spout again.	Touch thumb of one hand to index finger of other hand and switch back and forth as you raise arms.

It's fun to act out this rhyme with props. Purchase a small piece of waterspout (downspout) from the hardware store, a spider (a spider glove puppet is great, or look for a small plastic spider at Halloween), and a watering can to be used for make-believe rain. Make a sun from yellow posterboard with a circle cut from the middle for a child's head. Assign parts: one child moves the spider up the spout, another child pretends to pour the rain as the spider is washed out, and the spider climbs up again as the sun comes out. (Or use a tall stool as the spout and let a child pretend to be the spider!) Be prepared to sing the rhyme over and over until each child has had a turn to play a part. Leave the props out so that children can enjoy singing the rhyme all by themselves.

Write the rhyme on chart paper and laminate. Call out words or letters and have children come up and circle their selections with a wipe-off marker. On different days, work on different phonics skills and language conventions, such as circling the periods, circling words with short vowel sounds, circling blends, and underlining a word that rhymes with *itsy*.

Write the rhyme on sentence strips and place them in a pocket chart. Draw pictures for some of the following key words or use the pictures on pages 268–272: *spider, up, waterspout, rain, sun, down.* As you read the rhyme with the class, stop at the pictures and have the class say the word. Encourage children to place the pictures over the words in the pocket chart. Take the sentence strips out of the pocket chart and encourage individuals or small groups to put the sentence strips in order on the floor.

Cut these felt shapes for your flannel board to illustrate the song: a black spider, blue raindrops, a brown or gray L-shaped waterspout, and a yellow sun. Add the pieces to the flannel board as you sing the song. Leave the pieces out so that individual children can manipulate the pieces as they sing. (These pieces are also available commercially.)

Choose a color and shape for each of the nouns in the rhyme (suggestions follow). Then do one or more of the following projects: make individual accordion-fold books for each child, illustrate the song with the shapes on the flannel board, make an individual flannel board from a cigar box (see page 81 for directions), or make a book for the class using the shapes.

spider	small black circle
water spout	gray rectangle
sun	large yellow circle
raindrops	small blue triangles

Page 1

The itsy, bitsy spider climbed up the water spout.

black oval at top of gray rectangle

Page 2

Down came the rain and washed the spider out.

black oval at bottom of gray rectangle, three blue triangles

Page 3

Out came the sun and dried up all the rain.

yellow circle in left corner, black oval at bottom of gray rectangle

Page 4

And the itsy, bitsy spider climbed up the spout again.

same as Page 1

The itsy bitsy spider climbed up the water spout

Down came the rain and washed the spider out

Out came the sun and dried up all the rain

And the itsy bitsy spider climbed up the spout again

Encourage children to make their own reproductions of this poem. Write words for each of the pages. The general format follows.

Page 1: A spider climbing up a water spout

Page 2: Rain coming down

Page 3: The sun coming out and a rainbow

Page 4: The spider climbing back up the water spout

Have each child add a cover and the title "The Itsy Bitsy Spider" by (Child's Name). Bind books and send them home.

This is an excellent song for practicing sequencing skills. Use pictures drawn on index cards by children, make simple line drawings, or photocopy the pictures on pages 268–272. Practice the sequence with the group, then place all the pictures on one sheet of paper and photocopy for children to cut apart and sequence. Encourage children to take the sequence set home to show families.

By all means, find the cassette *For All Children* (Walt Disney, 1991) and enjoy Little Richard's version of "Itsy Bitsy Spider." Purchase of this audio cassette benefits the Pediatric AIDS Foundation. Children adore this modern interpretation of a childhood favorite. Even your quietest child will move to this music!

You must read and sing Iza Trapani's beautifully illustrated *The Itsy Bitsy Spider* to the children (Whispering Coyote Press, 1993), which starts with the original rhyme and then has its own adaptations. Encourage children to write and illustrate their own new verses.

 Be sure to find Joanne Oppenheim's *Eency Weency Spider* (Bantam Books, 1991), which includes the rhyme of the spider's adventure but also involves Little Miss Muffet, Humpty Dumpty, and Jack in the adventures. Children will enjoy seeing some of their favorite characters dance through this book!

 Look for die-cut spider and spider web note pads (Carson Dellosa, Shapes Etc., and Frank Schaffer). These individual sheets can be laminated and used as flashcards for practicing the alphabet, name recognition, numbers, number words, color words, sight or Dolch words, and spelling words.

 Individual die-cut spiders or web-shaped note pad sheets can be backed with tagboard, laminated, hole-punched around the perimeter, and used as individual lacing cards. Use a black or white shoelace for lacing or look for spider web laces, available around Halloween. Send a lacing card home with each child for practice.

 If students need more practice with lacing, purchase white plastic needle-point canvas. Cut pieces of canvas into spider-web shapes. Give children large plastic needles threaded with black yarn and have them sew in and out and all around. Each spider's web is different!

Make your own black play dough this week to encourage children to make spiders. Look for black food *paste* which you will find with cookie- and cake-decorating supplies. Liquid food coloring will not produce a true black, but play dough made with black food paste will be as black as night. Black food paste is especially easy to find around Halloween. Use the following "tried-and-true" play dough recipe.

2 c white all-purpose flour

1 c salt

4 tsp cream of tartar

black food paste

1 c water (add food paste to water)

2 Tb vegetable oil

Mix dry ingredients in a medium pot. Add wet ingredients. Cook over medium heat and stir until dough forms a big lump and pulls away from the sides of the pot. Store in an airtight container.

Encourage children to paint spiders this week by supplying black paint at the easel. Demonstrate painting a spider to the class by painting two circles or ovals (one large, one small) for the body and head and then adding eight legs. Gummed reinforcements make nice eyes.

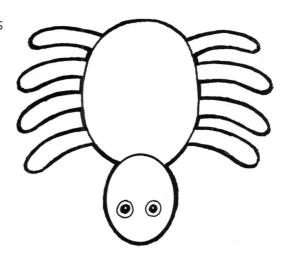

Plastic (Halloween) spiders or Mylar spider confetti (found with party supplies) can be added to your water table or to your sandbox for hours of fun.

 Use black spider-shaped confetti to make a sparkling water bottle. Peel the label off a clear-plastic bottle and fill three-quarters full of water. Add a small handful of spider-shaped confetti and some white Easter grass or white shredded-plastic package stuffing for webs. For a little sparkle, add silver or iridescent glitter. Hot-glue the cap onto the bottle so children will not be tempted to take it off and dump the contents! Float this spectacular water bottle in your water table or just let children enjoy tilting it back and forth and watching the spiders. Challenge children to get all the spiders into one end.

 Bring in a real house or garden spider for children to observe. Put the spider in a large jar with a piece of pantyhose stretched over the top, secured with a rubber band (or use a nail to punch holes in the lid). Add leaves and some wet sponge pieces. The spider will need two flies or mealworms per day (check your local pet store). Use a water mister to lightly mist the spider's habitat once a week. Make sure children understand that spiders are really helpful because they eat other insects, but caution children not to pick up spiders. Spiders do bite, and some children may have an allergic reaction. Alternatively, bring one or more spiders in for a day and put them in your aquarium or in a glass jar. Take children to a garden area with you to let the spiders go before children go home for the day.

Learn some facts about real spiders by reading books about spiders to the class. Choose from some of the following titles or ask your librarian for suggestions.

Cole, Joanna. *Spider's Lunch: All About Garden Spiders*. Grosset and Dunlap, 1995.

Gibbons, Gail. *Spiders*. Holiday House, 1993.

Graham, Margaret. *Be Nice to Spiders*. Harper & Row, 1978.

Jones, Cherrill. *Easy Theme Readers: Spiders*. Teacher Created Materials, 1996.

Podendorf, Illa. *Spiders: A New True Book*. Childrens Press, 1982.

After you have read some books about spiders, make a list of important facts about spiders. Here are some to get you started.

Spiders catch flies in their webs to eat.

Spiders spin webs with their spinnerets.

Spiders have eight legs.

Spiders have two body parts.

Spiders have fangs.

Most spiders have eight eyes.

Spiders lay eggs.

Spiders are arachnids.

Spiders live wherever they can find food.

Spiders have no bones.

There are four kinds of spider webs.

Or make a spider "web" using the information on page 182. Draw a large spider and put one fact on each of the eight legs or look for a commercial spider chart to write the facts on.

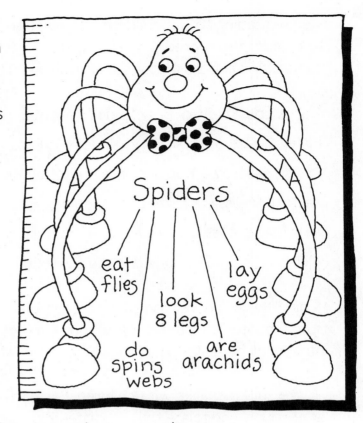

Spiders

eat flies

look 8 legs

lay eggs

do spins webs

are arachids

 Use this same information to make up a chant with children.

This is what the spiders eat, spiders eat, spiders eat.

This is what the spiders eat.

Spiders eat flies!

This is how the spiders look, spiders look, spiders look.

This is how the spiders look.

Spiders have eight legs!

You and the children can make up other verses after doing your research and making your web. As you chant each verse, keep a steady beat by hitting the palms of your hands on the tops of your thighs.

 Children will enjoy singing "There Was An Old Woman Who Swallowed a Fly" about the woman who swallowed a fly and then swallowed a spider to catch the fly. A wonderful book illustrating this song is Pam Adams' *There Was an Old Lady Who Swallowed a Fly* (Child's Play, 1996).

Enjoy reading to the children some fiction stories featuring spiders. Be sure to let them predict what the story will be about and identify the title, author, and illustrator. Glean facts about spiders as you read.

Carle, Eric. *The Very Busy Spider*. Philomel, 1984.

Haley, Gail. *A Story, A Story*. Aladdin, 1988.

Joosse, Barbara M. *Spiders in the Fruit Cellar*. Knopf, 1983.

Kajpust, Melissa. *A Dozen Silk Diapers*. Hyperion, 1993.

Kirk, David. *Miss Spider's Tea Party*. Scholastic, 1994.

McNulty, Faith. *The Lady and the Spider*. Harper & Row, 1986.

 Enjoy the video version of *Charlotte's Web* or simply read selections from Chapter 5 of the book, where Charlotte, who is a spider, introduces herself.

Make spider snacks with children. For each snack you will need two large round chocolate or chocolate-chip cookies, raisins or chocolate chips, eight short pretzel sticks or black licorice laces, and peanut butter. Spread peanut butter on one cookie. Stick the pretzels or licorice into the peanut butter so that they stick out to the sides like spider legs. Add the top cookie. For eyes, "glue" two chocolate chips to the top of the cookie with peanut butter. Let children try to make their own spider snacks on paper plates. The itsy bitsy spider crawled into my mouth. . . .

Splish-Splash Water Activities

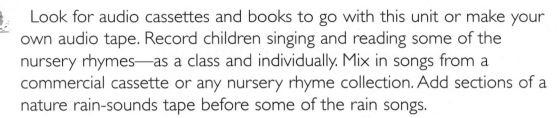

Look for audio cassettes and books to go with this unit or make your own audio tape. Record children singing and reading some of the nursery rhymes—as a class and individually. Mix in songs from a commercial cassette or any nursery rhyme collection. Add sections of a nature rain-sounds tape before some of the rain songs.

Put water in a bucket and add some large paintbrushes. Have children take the bucket outside and "paint" a playhouse or fence. Write numbers and letters, names and words with "disappearing paint."

Set up a water table or tub. Place a large beach towel under the tub to soak up the water. Add buckets, ladles, measuring cups, and other things that pour and measure water. Look for other interesting things to add to the water, such as funnels, corks, ping-pong balls, margarine tubs, clear-plastic bottles, squeeze bottles, sponge pieces, and a baster.

Add food coloring to your water table for fun! Make the water a different color each day! If you do not have a see-through water table, put colored water in clear-plastic bottles.

Set up sink-and-float activities at the water table.

Have a "Wet and Wild Water Day" to culminate this unit. Set up several water activities: a wading pool with marbles on the bottom and chairs all around (children sit in a chair with one shoe off and pick up the marbles with toes); bubbles with all different kinds of wands and blowers, including tin cans, bracelets, egg poachers, funnels, plastic six-pack rings, strawberry baskets; spray and squirt bottles filled with water. Consider having the children wear swimsuits and setting up a sprinkler.

Enjoy reading some of the following "splish-splash" books to your class. Show the covers and have children predict what each of the books is about. Discuss the books as you read.

Asch, Frank. *Water.* Harcourt Brace, 1995.

Berger, Melvin. *Amazing Water.* Newbridge, 1996 (big book and student six-pack).

Carlstrom, Nancy. *Better Not Get Wet, Jesse Bear.* Macmillan, 1988.

Cole, Joanna. *The Magic School Bus at the Waterworks.* Scholastic, 1986.

Graham, Joan Bransfield. *Splish Splash.* Ticknor & Fields, 1994.

Jonas, Ann. *Splash.* Greenwillow, 1995.

Kuhn, Dwight and Melvin Berger. *Bubbles, Bubbles, Everywhere.* Newbridge, 1996 (big book and student six-pack).

Leutscher, Alfred. *Water.* Dial, 1983.

Lindgren, Barbro. *Sam's Bath.* Morrow, 1983.

Murphy, Jill. *Five Minutes Peace.* Putnam, 1986.

Pollock, Penny. *Water Is Wet.* Putnam, 1985.

Watanabe, Shigeo. *I Can Take a Bath!* Philomel, 1986.

Watanabe, Shigeo. *Let's Go Swimming.* Philomel, 1990.

Schwartz, Alvin. *I Saw You in the Bathtub and Other Folk Rhymes.* HarperCollins, 1992.

YUM! YUM! RHYMES

Little Miss Muffet sat on a tuffet,
Eating her curds and whey.
Along came a spider who sat down beside her,
And frightened Miss Muffet away!

A traditional tune for this nursery rhyme can be found in Pamela Beall and Susan Nipp's *Wee Sing Nursery Rhymes and Lullabies* (Price, Stern & Sloan, 1985). The *Wee Sing* set comes with an audio cassette and sing-along book. It is easily found in most toy, book, or school-supply stores and can be ordered directly from Price, Stern & Sloan Publishers, Inc., 410 North La Cienega Boulevard, Los Angeles, CA 90048.

Practice chanting this rhyme while keeping a steady beat. After children have mastered clapping the beat, choose other motions, such as snapping fingers, hitting thighs with hands, moving one hand up and down, hitting hips, or tapping noses with index fingers.

Play out the rhyme for the class using a doll for Miss Muffet and a spider puppet. (Spooky Spider Glove Puppet can be ordered from Demco, Inc., Box 7488, Madison, Wisconsin 53707-7488, 1-800-356-1200, or look for spider glove puppets available around Halloween.) Large paper or rubber spiders work well, too. Use a box or bowl for the tuffet to sit the doll on and manipulate the characters as you say the rhyme. Leave the props out to encourage children to work with them independently.

This is a rhyme that children love to act out. You will need a bowl and spoon, a tuffet (stool or chair), and a spider. Choose one child to be Little Miss (or Mister) Muffet, who pretends to be eating curds and whey. Another child gets to manipulate the spider (or gets to *be* the spider, creeping up menacingly behind Miss Muffet!). When the spider appears behind Miss Muffet, she screams (the favorite part!) and runs away. Have the class recite the verse as two children ham it up. Be prepared to do it over and over so that each child has a turn. Substitute children's names in the verse ("Little *Maggie* Muffet . . .").

Make Miss Muffet puppets on craft sticks. Each child draws Miss Muffet, cuts around the drawing, and glues it to a stick. Drop a plastic spider on a string down beside Miss Muffet. Encourage children to use the stick puppets and spider with a puppet stage to act out the rhyme.

Look for small plastic spiders or spider rings—easy to find at Halloween (or order from Oriental Trading, P.O. Box 3407, Omaha, NE 68103-0407). Tie a string to each spider and then tie the string loosely to each child's finger. Have children bunch up the strings in their fists and drop the spider as they say the line "... along came a spider." Rehearse before children go home so that they can scare everyone in their house (while practicing the rhyme, of course!).

This rhyme has some vocabulary that may be unfamiliar to children. Find a picture of the rhyme in a nursery-rhyme collection or use the one on page 188. Mount the picture on tagboard and discuss what is happening in the picture with children. Label the vocabulary in the picture: *Miss Muffet, tuffet* (a low stool or grassy hill), *curds and whey* (a peasant's dessert much like cottage cheese), *spider*. Write these words with marker in the margins around the picture. Children will find other things in the picture to label that do not relate directly to the poem, which is fine. Each day, go over the words that the class has identified, pointing out those that relate to the rhyme. Encourage children to use magnetic letters to spell the identified words.

Write the rhyme on chart paper or look for a commercial chart with the rhyme. Draw pictures for some of the words on sticky notes or use the pictures of a tuffet, a spider, curds and whey, and Miss Muffet on pages 268–272. Encourage students to match the pictures to the words on the chart. Then say the rhyme with the class, stopping at the pictures to let children say the words. Hot-glue a rubber or plastic spider to the end of a dowel to use as a pointer that will keep children's attention. Point out individual words. The child who guesses the word first gets to come up and point to the next word. Leave the pointer out so that children will be encouraged to practice "reading" the rhyme individually.

Have each child draw or paint a reproduction of this rhyme. Accordion-fold tagboard into four sections. Prewrite or have child write one line of the poem on each section. Discuss each line and then invite children to draw their interpretations of the line. Children will love taking their books home to "read" to their families.

Little Miss Muffet sat on a tuffet,	little girl sitting on stool
Eating her curds and whey.	girl eating from bowl with spoon
Along came a spider who sat down beside her	girl with bowl and spider
And frightened Miss Muffet away!	bowl and spoon on ground, stool empty

Have each child illustrate the line . . . *along came a spider who sat down beside (child's name)* with a self-portrait, a spider, and any details the child wishes to add. Write the words (or have children write them) under each picture. Display the illustrations on a bulletin board with the title "Along Came a Spider." After children have enjoyed the pictures, take them down and bind them together for a class book.

Give each child a spider ring (available around Halloween) or a paper spider and have some fun while you work on position words. As you call out the sentences, children put their spiders in the appropriate places. Try these: the spider sat down *beside* her, *on top* of her head, on her *left* and *right* hands, *underneath* her knee, *inside* her hand, *behind* her back, and so on. Challenge children to think up others.

This is a wonderful rhyme to sequence. Look for sequence cards, make your own with simple line drawings on index cards, or find a series of pictures in a nursery-rhyme book. Three cards are sufficient: 1) Miss Muffet sitting and eating, 2) the spider joining her, 3) Miss Muffet running away. Ask children what happened in the beginning, in the middle, and at the end.

Have children write an innovation for this rhyme. Brainstorm other things that might be scary, such as the dark, monsters, snakes, and bugs. Then let children decide which scary thing might fit into the lines of the rhyme. Lines 2 and 4 should rhyme.

Line 1—Someone sits somewhere.

Line 2—Eating something.

Line 3—Something scary shows up.

Line 4—Scary thing chases someone away.

Encourage children to illustrate any innovations they write. Here is one class's innovation.

Mrs. Timmons' class sat at their desks

Eating their snack one day.

Along came a snake who slithered beside them

And scared (child's name) away!

Have children make curds and whey the old-fashioned way. Curds and whey was a peasant's dessert—a treat that ended the meal. Bring 2 cups of whole milk to a boil. Watch carefully, because milk boils over easily. Take the pot off the burner and add one tablespoon of vinegar. Watch as the milk curdles. Put the mixture through a tea strainer to drain the liquid, which is the whey. What remains are the curds. Add 2–4 teaspoons of pancake syrup and give each child a little taste on the tip of a tongue depressor. You can also cut toast into quarters and spread with the curds.

Make a T-graph of the tasting experience with the title, "Do You Like Curds and Whey?" Yes answers go down the left side of the T and No answers go down the right. Give children clip clothespins so they can clip their answers on the appropriate side. Discuss the results.

Do you like curds and whey?

Explain to children that curds and whey is much like our modern cottage cheese. Have cottage cheese over canned pineapple tidbits for a simpler version of curds and whey.

Learn these words to the tune of "The Angel Band."

> There was one, there were two, there were three little spiders,
>
> There were four, there were five, there were six little spiders,
>
> There were seven, there were eight, there were nine little spiders,
>
> Ten little spiders scaring me!
>
> Oh, wasn't that a day with Miss Muffet, with Miss Muffet, with Miss Muffet?
>
> Wasn't that a day with Miss Muffet?
>
> That spider scared me, too!

Use ten fingers to sing the song, clapping to a steady beat for the second verse. Place a spider ring on each finger as you lead the song. Then choose a child to be the leader and wear the rings.

Have children make individual books that illustrate the song. Photocopy the words on pages in advance or have children write them. Children make thumbprint spiders with a washable black inkpad (one thumbprint for one spider, two thumbprints for two spiders, and so on). After all the thumbprints are made, children add eight legs and two eyes to each spider with a fine-tipped black marker.

10 little spiders in the web!

Children enjoy the count-down (10 to 1) rhyme about spiders by Rozanne Lanczak Williams, *Spiders, Spiders Everywhere!* (Creative Teaching Press, 1995) available in big book and individual student books.

Here are some interesting facts about spiders and webs.

Spiders use spinnerets, which are at the ends of their bodies and produce a silky thread, to make their webs.

Liquid emerges from the spinnerets and hardens as it touches the air.

The most familiar web is the orb. Orb webs are round, like bicycle wheels.

Spiders wait as insects fly into their webs and get caught in the sticky web.

Although many spiders have lots of eyes, they do not see well, so they depend on their sensitivity to touch to let them know when they have caught their dinner.

When the insect is caught, the spider uses a bite from its fangs to paralyze it.

The spider wraps the insect in silk thread until the spider is ready to eat.

Baby spiders are called spiderlings.

A mother spider encloses her eggs in a silken sac.

Help children make spider-web paintings with black paint on white paper. Like real spider webs, each will be unique. Put the white paper into the lid of a shirt box. Put black tempera paint and 3–6 marbles in a cup. Scoop the marbles out of the cup with a slotted spoon and place them on the white paper in the box lid. Children roll the marbles around the lid to form weblike lines. Read Eric Carle's *The Very Busy Spider* (Philomel Books, 1984), in which children can actually feel the web as it is built by the busy spider. Look for the big book *Spider Webs* by Christine Back and Barrie Watts (Modern Curriculum Press, 1994) with dramatic photographs showing a spider actually making a web.

Children may wish to add spiders to the webs they painted. If so, use the gumballs that fall from sweet gum trees, if available, or large black pompoms. Black pipe cleaners make nice spider legs. Use a low-temperature hot glue gun and help children glue on two plastic wiggle eyes and eight legs. Pipe cleaners fit nicely into the gumball holes but will still need a little glue to hold them tightly. Or cross four black pipe cleaners under the bottom of a pompom, attach with hot glue and bend to look like spider legs. Display the webs and spiders on a bulletin board with the title "Relaxing After a Good Scare!"

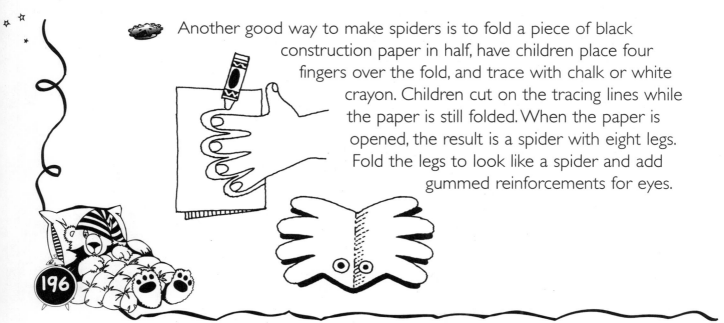

Another good way to make spiders is to fold a piece of black construction paper in half, have children place four fingers over the fold, and trace with chalk or white crayon. Children cut on the tracing lines while the paper is still folded. When the paper is opened, the result is a spider with eight legs. Fold the legs to look like a spider and add gummed reinforcements for eyes.

🕷 Display children's spiders and webs around a copy of Shel Silverstein's poem "The Weavers" from *Falling Up* (HarperCollins, 1994).

🕷 Look for plastic spiders (easily found around Halloween, or order from Oriental Trading, P.O. Box 2308, Omaha, NE 68103-2308, 1-800-228-2269). Put a different number of these in a see-through estimating jar each day and challenge children to guess how many they see. Write down each child's guess on a sticky note (look for spider sticky-note pads!) and attach to the jar. At the end of the day, dump the spiders and count them in front of the children. The child with the correct guess gets to pass out a small treat to the rest of the class.

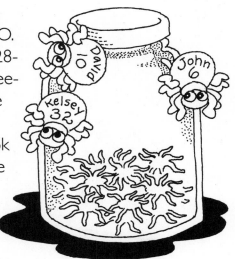

🕷 Use the same plastic spiders to make a counting game. With a black marker, draw webs on white tagboard or large white unlined index cards. Write a number from 1 to 10 or from 1 to 20 on each card. Children count the appropriate number of spiders onto each card.

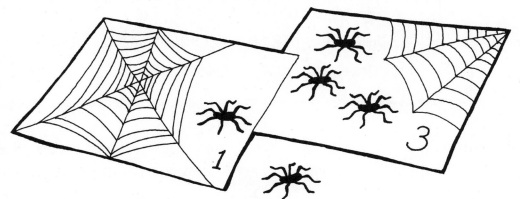

🕷 Use the plastic spiders to teach children to play "drop the spider." Put a bowl (Miss Muffet's bowl) behind a chair. Have each child take a handful of plastic spiders and kneel on the seat of the chair, facing backwards. Children try to drop spiders into the bowl. The child who gets the most spiders to stay in the bowl wins. Have children practice simple addition by taking two or three turns and adding their scores together for a grand total.

Little Jack Horner sat in a corner
Eating his Christmas pie.
He put in his thumb and pulled out a plum
And said, "What a good boy am I!"

A traditional tune for this nursery rhyme can be found in Pamela Beall and Susan Nipp's *Wee Sing Nursery Rhymes and Lullabies* (Price, Stern & Sloan, 1985). The *Wee Sing* set comes with an audio cassette and sing-along book. It is easily found in most toy, book, or school-supply stores or can be ordered directly from Price, Stern & Sloan Publishers, Inc., 410 North La Cienega Boulevard, Los Angeles, CA 90048.

Have individual children act out this rhyme as the class recites it. The child will need a small chair or stool, a pie tin, a spoon or fork, and a plum (a ball of purple play dough rolled into a ball). Encourage each child to go through the motions of pretending to eat Christmas pie, putting in a thumb, pulling out the thumb with the purple plum, and saying, "What a good boy (girl) am I!" Leave the props out at a play-dough center so children can make plum pie and recite the poem during the day.

Write the rhyme on chart paper and laminate. Practice phonics skills and language conventions by asking children to come up and use a purple wipe-off marker to circle words that rhyme, circle specific words, underline capital letters, circle quotation marks, and put X's on words with short vowel sounds. Count the number of words in the rhyme (29!).

Read the rhyme with the class, using a pointer (a plastic pie server, plastic knife, or wooden spoon) to touch each word as you read. Use cloze occasionally by saying the first part of a line and letting children supply the last word. For example, *Teacher*: "Little Jack Horner sat in a . . ." *Children*: "Corner!" Use the same cloze method with each line.

Practice the rhyme by replacing *Jack* with the name of each child in the class ("Little *Kelsey* Horner sat in a corner"). Children delight in hearing their own names. Each time you say the rhyme, be sure the child pretends to put in a thumb and pull out a plum.

Find a picture of the rhyme in a nursery-rhyme collection or use the illustration on page 198. Mount the picture on tagboard and laminate. With the class, label the vocabulary in the picture (*Jack, corner, pie, plum*). Children will find other things in the picture to label that do not relate directly to the poem, which is fine. Go over the words that the class has identified each day, pointing out those that relate to the rhyme.

Encourage children to memorize "Little Jack Horner." Give children a sticker (nursery-rhyme sticker, purple gummed dot found with office supplies, or simply a purple dot "plum" made with purple marker) when they memorize the rhyme.

Have each child write an innovation of the poem by filling in the blanks.

Little _____ Horner

Sat in a corner

Eating his (her) _____ pie.

He (she) put in his (her) thumb

And pulled out a _____

And said, "What a good boy (girl) am I!"

Use sticky notes to place new words over the original words on the chart and read each new rhyme with the class. Encourage children to illustrate their new rhymes. Display the illustrations and new verses on purple construction paper.

Make a class book by photocopying each child's hand on the photocopy machine. Place each hand palm down—four fingers together, thumb out. Cut out the prints. Then have children illustrate the line "(Child's name) put in his/her thumb and pulled out a _____!" On sheets of white paper, children draw whatever they wrote in the blank, cut it out, and glue it on top of their photocopied thumb. Add a brown construction-paper pie, if desired. Write the completed sentence at the bottom of each hand picture and mount on purple construction paper. Bind the pictures together to make a class book. For the cover, take an instant photo of the class holding up purple play-dough plums on their thumbs!

Bryanna put in her thumb and pulled out a baby doll.

Put a little purple circle on the tip of every child's fingers with washable marker. Then say the poem, adapting the second-to-last line to review numbers.

> Little Jack Horner sat in a corner
>
> Eating his Christmas pie.
>
> He stuck in his thumb and pulled out (number) plums
>
> And said, "What a good boy am I!"

Children hold up the appropriate number of purple fingers as you call each number. It's not necessary to do this in numerical order. Invite each child to take a turn leading the verse and calling his or her favorite number.

Encourage children to make their own books to illustrate this adaptation. Preprint the words for each number or have children write their own. Have children use a fingertip or a cork dipped in purple paint or a purple bingo dabber for the appropriate number of purple plums next to each number sentence.

He put in his thumb and pulled out 1 plum
●

He put in his thumb and pulled out 2 plums
● ●

He put in his thumb and pulled out 3 plums
● ● ●

Cut some pie shapes from brown construction paper. On the crust of each pie, glue some purple circles to represent plums—a different number on each pie. Flash the pies and have children say the poem with the appropriate number in it.

> Little Jack Horner sat in a corner
>
> Eating his Christmas pie.
>
> He put in this thumb and pulled out (number) plums
>
> And said, "What a good boy am I!"

Use purple play dough this week at your play-dough center. Add small tart tins, (like the ones that come with pot pies) or regular-sized pie pans. Encourage children to make "plum pies" by rolling balls of dough (plums) and putting them in the pie tins. Add a rolling pin and show children how to roll out dough to make pie crust. Ask children to put in a thumb and pull out a plum.

Let each child make a pie by hiding a "plum" (purple bouncy ball, large purple macramé bead, or large purple stringing bead) in a disposable pie tin and then spraying shaving cream all over the top. Then, pull out the plum by searching through the shaving cream! Paint smocks are advisable. This can be done outside, too—use a water hose for cleanup.

Make Little Jack Horner thumbprint plum pies.

1 c butter or margarine, softened	2/3 c sugar
1/2 tsp salt	1 tsp vanilla
2 egg yolks	2 c flour
plum jam	

Cream butter and sugar together. Add salt, vanilla, and egg yolks and beat well. Add flour and blend well. Wrap dough in plastic wrap and refrigerate. This can be done prior to class if you wish. Give each child a tablespoon of dough. Have children shape the dough into a ball and then press a thumbprint into the center. Place the thumbprint balls on an ungreased cookie sheet and have children fill their indentations with plum jam. Bake for 20 minutes at 300 degrees F.

Draw and color a pie on 10 or 20 pieces of tagboard or large index cards (or cut pies from brown construction paper and glue to tagboard). Number the cards from 1 to 10 or from 1 to 20. Use purple pompoms or small purple stringing beads for counters. Or try a class favorite—purple magnetic bingo chips. Buy the transparent plastic chips with metal rims. The bingo chips come with a magnetic "magic wand" that attracts the metal rims. After children have placed the appropriate number of plums on each pie, they can use the wand to "pull out" the plums.

To practice matching, cut out 18 to 20 Little Jack Horner gingerbread-style boys from construction paper. Use wallpaper samples, fabric, or wrapping paper to make pairs of matching vests to fit the construction-paper boys. To make the game seasonal, use seasonal wrapping paper or festive fabric. For a simpler version, use construction paper and have children match colored vests. For a more difficult game, put uppercase letters on some and lowercase letters on others (or have children match colors to color words, numerals to sets, alphabet letters to initial/ending consonant sounds.) Put the boys out on a table in the corner and call the game "Little Jack Horner's Matching Corner."

Bring in a plum for each child for snack (a parent may be willing to send these in). Save the plum stones and tape to sentence strips that say, "(Child's name) ate a plum today." If plums are unavailable, bring in plum jelly or jam and spread it on minirice cakes or toast cut into circles with a biscuit cutter for miniplum pies.

Make a T-graph after all the children have had a chance to taste a plum. On the top of a T-shaped strip of tagboard, write the question, "Do you like plums?" On one side of the top of the T, write the word *yes* and draw a smiley face. One the other side, write the word *no* and draw a sad face. Invite each child to clip a clothespin on the side that represents his or her response. Make sure to include a clothespin for yourself. When you have finished, ask children to decide which side has the most and which side has the least.

Use the letters **P-L-U-M** to make an acrostic poem. Mount the poems on purple construction-paper circles.

Purple plum

Looks delicious

Unusually good

M-m-m-m!

Pease porridge hot,
Pease porridge cold.
Pease porridge in the pot, nine days old.

Some like it hot,
Some like it cold.
Some like it in the pot, nine days old!

A traditional tune for this nursery rhyme can be found in Pamela Beall and Susan Nipp's *Wee Sing Nursery Rhymes and Lullabies* (Price, Stern & Sloan, 1985). The *Wee Sing* set comes with an audio cassette and sing-along book. It is easily found in most toy, book, or school-supply stores or can be ordered directly from Price, Stern & Sloan Publishers, Inc., 410 North La Cienega Boulevard, Los Angeles, CA 90048.

Teach children this rhyme while clapping a steady beat. More mature children will enjoy the hand-clapping game that goes with this rhyme. In earlier years, school children played this game to help keep their hands warm on cold days. Partners face each other and repeat this sequence as they say the rhyme: clap own hands; clap right hands together with partner; clap own hands; clap left hands together with partner; clap own hands; clap both hands together with partner's hands. The sequence immediately repeats. After children have confidence in the sequence, they can repeat it faster each time until one of the players breaks the sequence through laughter or exhaustion!

Have children sit in a circle with you. When you lift your arm up high, children shout the rhyme. When you hold your arm in the middle, children say the rhyme in a normal tone. When you have your hand on the floor, children whisper the rhyme. Move your hand up and down and have children follow your lead with their voices. Then choose a child to be the leader.

Write the rhyme on chart paper and laminate. Invite children to circle certain letters, sight words, words that begin with certain letters, and words that rhyme; put a line in all the spaces between words; underline capital letters; put an X on words with short vowels; circle commas; and so on.

Have children circle all the words that begin with the letter *p* (*pease, porridge, pot*) on the laminated chart. Divide children into small groups. Give each group three minutes to think of all the words they can that begin with *p*.

After children have learned the rhyme, challenge them with this riddle (from 1765!).

Pease porridge hot,

Pease porridge cold.

Pease porridge in the pot,

Nine days old.

Spell me that without a P,

And a clever scholar you will be.

The riddle of course, is that the rhyme says "spell me *that* without a P." The answer is *T-H-A-T!* Once children "get it," they will enjoy taking it home and trying it out on their families.

Teach children the tongue twister, "Peter Piper Picked a Peck of Pickled Peppers."

Peter Piper picked a peck of pickled peppers.

A peck of pickled peppers Peter Piper picked.

If Peter Piper picked a peck of pickled peppers,

Where's the peck of peppers Peter Piper picked?

Write this tongue twister on chart paper and laminate, or make individual copies for each child. Have children circle all the words in this tongue twister that begin with the letter *P*. Look for books of tongue twisters, such as Joanna Cole and Stephanie Calmenson's *Six Sick Sheep: 101 Tongue Twisters* (Morrow Junior Books, 1993). Try a different tongue twister each day.

Have each child come up with a tongue twister of no more than five words for their own name. For example,

Courtney caught a copper-colored codfish.

Wesley went to water the wilting wildflowers.

Help children write their tongue twisters on sentence strips and display them in the room. Challenge children to say the tongue twisters five times fast. Can you do it? Each morning, choose one tongue twister to try, making sure that children identify the letter they hear most often and that they identify the words that begin with that letter.

Expand the tongue twisters, using the format from "Peter Piper."

Use the child's first-name sentence for the first line (see above).

For the second line, use the same words but turn the sentence around.

The third line is the first line but starts with *if*.

The fourth line is a question, starting with "Where . . ."

Wesley went to water the wilting wildflowers.

The wilting wildflowers Wesley went to water.

If Wesley went to water the wilting wildflowers,

Where are the wilting wildflowers that Wesley went to water?

Have children use the format to write their own "first name" tongue twisters. Bind the verses together to make a class book of tongue twisters. Have children illustrate their tongue twisters at the tops of the pages and write them at the bottoms.

Pease is an old way of spelling the plural of *pea*. Pease porridge is a pea soup. Have children shell fresh peas and then make their own pease porridge. Ask children if they would really like "pease porridge in the pot nine days old."

Pease Porridge

peas (fresh, dried, or frozen)

any cream soup (split pea, cream of mushroom, creamy chicken mushroom)

Precook the peas. Drain off the liquid and add to the cream soup.

Save one bowl of pease porridge. Put the bowl in an old aquarium for nine days or until you can't stand it anymore! Have children keep a journal by drawing and writing about the changes that they see each day. Would anyone want to eat it after nine days?

Select fresh green peas in pods that can be shelled. Give each child one pod and ask him or her to predict how many peas will be in the pod. Then have children shell the peas to see if their predictions were correct. Graph the number of peas in each pod by writing numbers across the bottom of a piece of tagboard. Give each child a paper pea pod to put above the number that tells how many peas were in his or her pod. Discuss the graph.

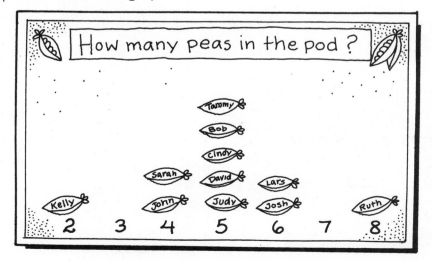

For each child, fold a sheet of paper into four or eight squares. Have children write or trace a number in each square. Then invite them to use a green bingo dabber to dab the appropriate number of green "peas" in each square.

Cut pea-pod shapes from green posterboard. Put a number on each pea pod and laminate. Challenge children to count the appropriate number of peas onto each pod. For peas, you can use any large dried pea (black-eyed peas, yellow eye peas), small green pompoms, green stringing beads, or green plastic bingo chips.

Sit children on the floor and teach them this rhyme from our oral tradition.

Five little peas in a pea pod pressed.	Make a fist.
One grew,	Pop out little finger.
Two grew,	Pop out ring finger.
So did the rest.	Pop out each of the other fingers and thumb one at a time.
They grew and they grew And they grew and never stopped.	Face palms together and make space bigger and bigger.
They grew so fat that the pea pod POPPED!	Jump up on POPPED!

Replace the sand in your sand table with dried peas. To fill the table, ask each family to send in one bag of any type of dried peas (black-eyed peas, yellow eye peas, green split peas, yellow split peas). Add some pouring and measuring cups, funnels, and various containers. Note: this is not for very young children who still put things in their ears or noses!

Buy a package of dried peas (choose the largest type in your grocery store so they will be easy for children to pick up). Write each child's name in pencil on a sentence strip. Have children trace over each letter—one at a time—with white glue and then place peas on the glue lines. Display the names around a copy of the following traditional poem.

I eat my peas with honey.

I've done it all my life.

It makes the peas taste funny

But it keeps them on the knife!

Pat-a-cake, pat-a-cake, baker's man,
Bake me a cake as fast as you can!
Roll it and pat it
And mark it with a B
And put in the oven for baby and me.

A traditional tune for this nursery rhyme can be found in Pamela Beall and Susan Nipp's *Wee Sing Nursery Rhymes and Lullabies* (Price, Stern & Sloan, 1985). The *Wee Sing* set comes with an audio cassette and sing-along book. It is easily found in most toy, book, or school-supply stores or can be ordered directly from Price, Stern & Sloan Publishers, Inc., 410 North La Cienega Boulevard, Los Angeles, CA 90048.

Photocopy the illustration on page 212, color it, and mount it on a large piece of tagboard. With the class, label the vocabulary in the picture (*baby, baker man, cake, B, oven*). Children will find other things to label that do not relate directly to the poem, which is fine. Go over the words that the class has identified each day, pointing out those that relate specifically to the rhyme.

Say the rhyme for each child in the class, changing the last two lines to use each child's name and initial. For example, ". . . and mark it with an *R*, and put in the oven for *Ryan* and me."

" . . . and mark it with a *B*." Fill a tub with flour (you may wish to do this outside or on an old shower curtain or sheet). In the flour hide alphabet-shaped pasta or, for less of a challenge, alphabet-shaped cookie cutters. Invite each child to come and find the first letter of his or her name (or the entire name).

Practice chanting this rhyme with children. After chanting is mastered, use motions to keep a steady beat. Clap hands, snap fingers, hit thighs, stomp feet, tap knees, and pat heads.

As with "Pease Porridge," more mature children will enjoy hand-clapping this rhyme. Two children face each other and as they say the rhyme, they repeat the clapping sequence on page 206. Try this variation for children who master the sequence: clap own hands; clap right hands together with partner; clap own hands; clap left hands together with partner; clap own hands; hit both thighs with both hands; and repeat.

Using the alphabet as your guide, help children brainstorm a list of kinds of cakes from apple spice cake to zoo cake. Combine all the lists the next day, including *all* the possibilities.

Encourage children to design their own cakes using markers, crayons, paint, and colored construction paper. Brainstorm the possibilities: chocolate cake, birthday cake, wedding cake, strawberry cake, valentine cake, Halloween cake, and so on. Below each cake, write the rhyme, "Pat-a-cake, pat-a-cake, _____ cake," filling in the blank with the type of cake each child chooses. Display the cakes on a bulletin board entitled "Pat-a-cake." To make cakes, provide a cake-shaped stencil for children to trace and cut from construction paper. Doilies cut in half make nice cake plates. Put out sequins, buttons, beads, rickrack, ribbon, pipe cleaners, and markers so that children can design cakes to go with their completed sentences.

Pat-a-cake,
pat-a-cake,
birthday cake.

Write the rhyme on chart paper and laminate. Children may use washable markers to mark letters, sight words, words that begin with certain letters, words that rhyme, capital letters, words with short vowels, spaces between words, commas, or whatever you choose.

Write the entire rhyme on sentence strips. Have children match the sentence strips to the lines of the laminated rhyme. Challenge individual or small groups of children to put the sentence strips in the correct order.

After children have enjoyed the sentence strips, have them watch you cut them into individual words. Place the words in order in a pocket chart and read the rhyme together with the class. Have children close their eyes, and choose one child to turn one word backwards. Children open their eyes and try to guess the mystery word. The child who guesses the word correctly takes the next turn.

Distribute the word cards to children. Display the rhyme on chart paper and help children recreate each line of the rhyme by bringing the words for that line up to the pocket chart or chalkboard ledge. Help children put the words in the correct order, using the chart for assistance. Read the line together and then go to the next one.

Look for commercial cake-shaped note pads in several sizes (especially birthday cakes and cupcakes) or simply cut your own cake shapes from colored construction paper to use for flashcards. Use the flashcards to practice numeral recognition; uppercase and lowercase letter recognition; Dolch, sight, and spelling words; and color and number words. Cake cards can also be used for matching activities: count birthday candles to match numerals on birthday cakes; match cupcakes with lowercase letters to larger cakes with uppercase letters; or match alphabet letters to pictures of initial consonant sounds. Adapt the cake cards to meet the skills needing practice in your classroom.

Have each child choose a letter of the alphabet and illustrate a cake for that letter on pages you have prepared (write the alphabet letter in the same spot on each page and add the name of the cake). Bind the cake pages together in alphabetical order to make a book entitled "Pat-a-cake, Pat-a-cake, Alphabet Cake!"

Encourage children to choose a cake from the alphabetical list to create with markers, crayons, colored construction paper, and a variety of decorations such as sequins, beads, rickrack, and ribbon. Have children complete the sentence *Pat-a-cake, pat-a-cake* _____ *cake* at the bottom of a sheet of colored construction paper. Provide cake-shaped stencils so children can trace and cut cakes from construction paper to glue down and decorate. Half a doily makes a nice cake plate!

For a no-bake version of the baker's cake, use a flavored rice cake for the cake and softened cream cheese or peanut butter for icing. Encourage children to decorate their own cakes with small candies, baking morsels, raisins, and so on. Suggest that children make their initials in the icing with candy pieces.

Consider making a real cake with your class. Choose any packaged cake mix or use your favorite "from scratch" recipe. Don't be too concerned about having a "perfect" cake or you'll forget to enjoy the process with the children. Be prepared for children to experiment with the ingredients. Have extra flour, sugar, and other ingredients available for children to "bake" with after you are done. You may wish to put a table outside for this play in order to keep flour off of *everything*!

Invite all the children to a tea party! Serve the cakes from one of the above activities and make tea using commercial tea bags—try some of the flavored versions. Offer sugar, lemon, or milk with the tea. Teach children the delightful nursery rhyme, "Polly Put the Kettle On." Children will enjoy acting out this rhyme with a tea kettle—two at a time—using their own names in place of Polly and Sukey.

Polly put the kettle on.	Sukey take it off again.
Polly put the kettle on.	Sukey take it off again.
Polly put the kettle on.	Sukey take it off again.
We'll all have some tea.	They've all gone away.

After showing children a teapot and making tea, teach them the fun children's song with motions, "I'm a Little Teapot."

I'm a little teapot, short and stout.	Bend knees.
Here is my handle,	Put one hand on waist.
Here is my spout.	Put other hand palm up, elbow bent.
When I get all steamed up,	
Hear me shout.	
Tip me over and pour me out.	Bend toward "spout" at waist.

Children will enjoy Iza Trapani's delightfully illustrated *I'm a Little Teapot* (Whispering Coyote Press, 1996), which begins with the original verse and goes on an entertaining journey with additional verses.

Yum! Yum! Activities

Make an audio cassette with the children. Record the class reading or singing the nursery rhymes in this unit. Then record some individuals saying or singing the rhymes as they are memorized and sprinkle in some commercial versions. Children love listening to themselves and each other.

Write the alphabet down the left side of a piece of chart paper. With children, brainstorm a list of foods that begin with each letter. Have volunteers illustrate the foods for each letter on a white paper plate or sheet of drawing paper. Write the letter at the bottom of each illustration. Put in alphabetical order and bind together with a ring binder.

Look for a copy of the nursery rhyme "A Apple Pie" which dates back to at least 1671. Many versions have been published. An older version is illustrated by Kate Greenaway, but children will really enjoy the updated comical fold-out version illustrated by Tracey Campbell Pearson (Dial Books for Young Readers, 1986). The rhyme uses verbs in alphabetical order telling of the things you can do with apple pie ("A apple pie . . . B bit it . . . C cut it . . . D dropped it. . . .") After reading the book, have each child choose a letter of the alphabet to illustrate for a class reproduction. Use the words from the book for each letter, if you wish. Put the pictures in alphabetical order with a cover to make a class big book. Enjoy reading the reproduction while making and eating apple pie!

Another fun nursery rhyme about apple pies is this one.

> If all the world were apple pie,
>
> And all the seas were ink,
>
> And all the trees
>
> Were bread and cheese,
>
> What would we have to drink?

Invite children to brainstorm a list of things that would be fun to drink in this strange apple-pie land! Encourage each child to illustrate this rhyme. Display the illustrations on a bulletin board around a copy of the rhyme.

Here's another nursery rhyme about food.

> Little Tommy Tucker
>
> Sings for his supper.
>
> What shall we give him?
>
> Brown bread and butter.

Have children write their own innovations of this rhyme using the same format.

> Little (child's name) Tucker
>
> Sings for his/her supper.
>
> What should we give him/her?
>
> _____ .

Encourage children to fill in the blank and illustrate their new verses. Display with the new words on a bulletin board.

Another favorite nursery rhyme is the standard "Hot Cross Buns."

Hot cross buns!
Hot cross buns!
One a penny, two a penny,
Hot cross buns!

Hot cross buns!
Hot cross buns!
If you have no daughters,
Give 'em to your sons.

Make hot cross buns for the class using any type of cinnamon bun, premade or from a mix. When the buns are cool, pipe on white icing in an X shape.

Teach children the favorite nursery song, "The Muffin Man."

Oh, do you know the muffin man, the muffin man, the muffin man?
Oh, do you know the muffin man who lives in Drury Lane?
Oh yes, I know the muffin man, the muffin man, the muffin man.
Oh yes, I know the muffin man who lives in Drury Lane.

Enjoy muffins—prepared, sent in by helpful parents, or made with the class. Any packaged mix is great—or use a favorite recipe. Have children write innovations of this rhyme, using characters from the nursery rhymes they learned in this unit.

Oh, do you know Little Jack Horner, Little Jack Horner,
   Little Jack Horner?
Oh, do you know Little Jack Horner, who ate his Christmas pie?

Oh, do you like pease porridge hot, pease porridge hot,
   pease porridge hot?
Oh, do you like pease porridge hot or do you like it cold?

Write the innovations on paper and have children illustrate their new rhymes. Encourage children to write other innovations by using characters from other rhymes they know.

Children will enjoy books about foods as they study these rhymes. Start by reading one of the many versions of *The Little Red Hen*, then go on to other stories that talk about food. Some suggestions follow.

Barton, Byron. *The Little Red Hen*. HarperCollins, 1993.

Ehlert, Lois. *Eating the Alphabet: Fruits and Vegetables A to Z*. Voyager, 1989.

Ehlert, Lois. *Growing Vegetable Soup*. Harcourt, Brace, 1987.

Falwell, Cathryn. *Feast for 10*. Clarion, 1993.

French, Vivian. *Oliver's Vegetables*. Orchard Books, 1995.

Galdone, Paul. *The Little Red Hen*. Seabury Press, 1973.

Hayes, Sarah. *Eat Up, Gemma*. Mulberry Books, 1988.

Speer-Lyon, Tammie. *Mother Goose's Kitchen*. Modern Publishing, 1996

STRANGE HOUSE RHYMES

There Was an Old Woman
Peter Peter Pumpkin Eater
The House That Jack Built
There Was a Crooked Man

There was an old woman who lived in a shoe.
She had so many children, she didn't know what to do.
So she gave them some broth without any bread
And spanked them all soundly and put them to bed.

If you object to "And spanked them all soundly . . .", substitute "And read them some stories . . ." or "And hugged them all tightly . . ." (children will still prefer *spanked!*).

Children will enjoy acting this rhyme out. Choose one child to be the old woman (or the old man). A bonnet or hat makes a nice prop but is not necessary. Decide what to use for a house—possibly a small table turned on its side or a large box. Add four or five children. Bowls and spoons are needed so that children can pretend to eat their broth. Then the old codger spanks each one (or hugs each one—children would rather spank!). Children lie down and pretend to sleep. Have the class recite the rhyme as the cast acts it out. Repeat until each child has had a turn to play a part.

Write the rhyme on chart paper. Consider using picture symbols for the words *woman, shoe, broth, bread, bed* (see pages 268–272). Write each of the pictured words on sticky notes and encourage children to match the words to the pictures.

Hot-glue a small plastic doll shoe to the end of a dowel and use this shoe pointer to point to each word as you say the rhyme. Leave the pointer out so that children will be encouraged to practice "reading" the rhyme with the pointer all by themselves.

Have children illustrate the rhyme. Show them several illustrations from nursery-rhyme collections, such as Greg Hildebrandt's *Mother Goose: A Treasury of Best-Loved Rhymes* (Platt and Munk Publishers, 1986), the cover of Elizabeth Murphy-Oliver's *Black Mother Goose* (Dare Books, 1981), or *One Two Buckle My Shoe: A Book of Counting Rhymes* by Rowan Barnes-Murphy (Little Simon, 1987). Have children draw the old woman and cut around their drawings so that they can be added to larger sheets, or have children find pictures of little old ladies in magazines. Supply several shoe stencils that children can choose from to represent the house, such as a boot, a tennis shoe, a high heel. Have children trace around the stencil onto colored construction paper of their choice and then cut out their shoe-shaped house. Add the old lady and the shoe to a larger sheet of construction paper. To represent the children, have children draw smiley faces (or use smiley-face stickers or rubber smiley-face stamps, or use colored dots that can be found with office supplies and add eyes and smiles).

Have children read some of the shoe books below to get ideas of other types of shoes. Children will especially enjoy Ann Morris, *Shoes Shoes Shoes* (Lothrop, Lee & Shepard, 1995), which opens with a real shoe-shaped house that was built to live in! The book also shows different kinds of shoes in photographs from around the world.

Look for Judy Nayen's beautifully illustrated *Who Wears Shoes?* (Newbridge, 1996), which comes as a big book and/or six-pack of student little books and a teacher's guide. Enjoy these other shoe books with your class.

Baily, Debbie. *Shoes.* Dominie Press, 1994.

Becker, Jennifer. *Shoes.* The Wright Group, 1991.

Dorros, Arthur. *Alligator Shoes.* Dutton, 1988.

Miller, Margaret. *Whose Shoe?* Greenwillow, 1991.

Wildsmith, Brian. *Whose Shoes?* Oxford University Press, 1987.

Introduce children to Shel Silverstein's "A Closet Full of Shoes" from *Falling Up* (HarperCollins, 1996). This poem lists all types of shoes. Have children volunteer to illustrate each pair of shoes mentioned in the poem. Then display the pictures on a bulletin board with a hand-written copy of the poem.

Establish some shoe categories based on the children's own shoes. Are they tie-up? Velcro? buckle? slip-on? Write each category across the bottom of a sheet of tagboard and add pictures cut from magazines or drawn by the children. Each child will need a marker for the chart—an instant photograph of his or her shoes, a sheet from a shoe-shaped note pad, a school photograph, or a tracing of his or her own shoe with name added. Working from the bottom of the chart up, invite each child to place a marker over the category that best fits his or her shoes. Be sure to add your own marker! Discuss the results.

Brainstorm a list of reasons why an old lady might want to live in a shoe! Then brainstorm a list of other places that she might want to live with her family. To give children some ideas, look for some innovations of this rhyme in "positive" Mother Goose adaptations (find the old lady who went to live in a sandal!) Let children write or draw adaptations of old ladies who live in a boot, a high heel, a tennis shoe, and so on. Look for Ken Hayes' *The Old Lady Who Lived Near the Zoo* (Newport Publishers, 1992), which comes with a minibook and audio cassette and is part of the "Nurture Rhymes for Special Times" series. This lady lives in a shoe near the zoo. Or *There Was an Old Lady Who Lived in a Glove* by Bernard Lodge (Whispering Coyote Press, 1992), which describes not only the glove house where the old woman lives but also other housing options (a flower, a hat, a pail). This may give children ideas for their own adaptions. Encourage children to illustrate their new verses.

> There was an old woman who lived in a boot.
>
> All her friends thought it was a hoot!
>
> There was an old woman who lived in a hat.
>
> Now tell me, what do you think of that!

Introduce Shel Silverstein's "Ickle Me, Pickle Me, Tickle Me, Too" from *Where the Sidewalk Ends* (HarperCollins, 1974). It's worth looking up just for the illustration. See if children can think of other things they could turn a shoe into!

 Make old woman's broth with the children.

> Old Woman's Broth
>
> 1/4 c sliced carrots
>
> 1/4 c sliced celery
>
> 2 cans condensed chicken broth or stock from one chicken boiled off the bone
>
> 1 soup can water
>
> 1 tsp parsley
>
> 1/4 tsp thyme

Have children dice and chop celery and carrots with plastic knives. Add all ingredients and bring to boil. Reduce heat and cover. Simmer for about 30 minutes. Serve the broth for snack as you say, "And the teacher gave them some broth with the best of her bread" (serve some bread sticks with the broth).

 Make a counting game from large index cards or tagboard cut to the appropriate size. Cut and glue a colorful shoe house on each card and write a number on each shoe. You will need 70 to 80 "children" for counters. Use large, dried lima beans—draw two eyes on each one with permanent marker. Have children count the appropriate number of "children" onto each shoe house.

Look for Gyo Fujikawa's *Original Mother Goose* (Grosset & Dunlap, 1968), which is a collection of nursery rhymes. In a double-page illustration of "There Was an Old Woman Who Lived in a Shoe," the shoe house actually has rooms. Use an overhead or opaque projector to enlarge a picture of a shoe house. Divide the house into rooms—living room, den, dining room, kitchen, bathroom, bedroom, laundry room, or attic. Add a porch off the back. Then have children cut from magazines pictures that fit into each of the rooms and add these pictures collage-style. Children might enjoy Richard Brown's *100 Words About My House* (Harcourt Brace Jovanovich, 1988) which will give children ideas for pictures to cut for each room.

 Discuss the parts of a shoe with the class: toe, heel, tongue, shoelaces, eyelet, sole. Have children identify each part on their own shoes. Not all shoes have all parts, of course. More mature students will enjoy Shel Silverstein's "Shoe Talk" from *Falling Up* (HarperCollins, 1996). Discuss how the author uses words related to shoes in his poem.

Look at the bottom of each child's shoe. Some shoes, especially rubber-soled tennis shoes, have very interesting designs. Show children how to put a piece of white bond paper over the bottom of the shoe (easier if the shoe is off) and make a rubbing of the bottom of the shoe using the side of a crayon. Have each child make at least one rubbing. Cut around rubbings and mount on brightly colored sheets of construction paper. Display on a bulletin board with the title, "Whose Shoes?" or "Put Your Best Foot Forward!"

Trevor's shoe

 Use sheets from shoe-shaped note pads to make flashcards. Laminate for durability. Practice uppercase and lowercase letter recognition, name recognition, numerals and number words, color words, and sight or Dolch words.

Have children make their own number shoe books. Precut shoe-shaped covers from construction paper and make ten white pages in the same shape for each book. Staple together. Children write one number from one to ten on each page. Then they cut shoes from magazines (you can precut shoe pictures for younger children) and glue the appropriate number of shoes on each numbered page. Be sure to include some shoe catalogs with your magazine supply.

To the tune of "Mary Had a Little Lamb," sing a song about the color of shoes each child is wearing. Go around the room and sing a verse for each child and the color of shoes he or she is wearing.

Kelly's wearing red shoes, red shoes, red shoes.

Kelly's wearing red shoes

And they are on her feet!

Make a class book of the song from the above activity. Take an instant photo of each child's shoes or cut shoe shapes of the appropriate color of construction paper for each child. Make shoe-shaped pages, if you wish. Write the child's verse under each photo and have children read the book as they sing the song. Add a cover that says, "Nobody Lives in My Shoes . . . But Me!"

John is wearing his white shoes
white shoes, white shoes
John is wearing his white shoes
And they are on his feet.

 Find an oversized pair of rubber boots. Lay out a long sheet of bulletin-board paper outside on a hard surface. Have each child take a turn walking first in a tray or tub of tempera paint and then on the paper. Start with a light color such as yellow. When that is used up, add red to the same tub, and finally orange (or yellow, blue, and green; or red, blue, and purple). Display the foot collage on a bulletin board with the words, "These Boots Were Made for Walking!" Consider taking photographs of the children as they make the banner to put around the display.

 This is a good time to see if children can lace and tie their own shoes. Use a pair of oversized adult shoes with easy eyelets and new shoelaces. Have each child put on the adult shoe over his or her own to practice lacing and tying.

 Children will enjoy the simple *My Lace-Up Book* by Kathie B. Smith (Nichols & Nickel Press, 1996), which has pictures of several different lace-up shoes and die-cut holes for lacing on each page. The book comes with a shoelace so that children can practice lacing on each of the board pages.

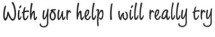 If children continue to have difficulty with shoe tying, ask them to bring in a shoebox. Supply each child with a long, colorful shoelace. Punch holes in the box top with a large nail to make holes for lacing and tying. To practice the rhyme, have children draw an old woman and make some paper-doll children to go on the outside of the shoebox house. Send the box home so that children can practice saying the rhyme and tying the shoelace with help from their parents. Attach the following poem.

There was an old woman who lived in a shoe.

She gave me this box to give to you.

Listen as I say my nursery rhyme

And then we'll spend just a little time.

With your help I will really try

To learn myself to lace and tie.

Peter Peter Pumpkin Eater
Had a wife and couldn't keep her,
Put her in a pumpkin shell
And there he kept her very well.

 To introduce this rhyme to your class, find a picture of the rhyme in a nursery-rhyme collection or use the illustration above. Mount the picture on a large piece of tagboard. With the class, label the vocabulary with a marker (*Peter, wife, pumpkin*) by drawing lines from each word out to the margins and printing the words. Children will find other things to label that do not relate directly to the poem, which is fine. Each day, go over the words that the class has identified, pointing out those that relate specifically to the rhyme.

Encourage children to memorize this traditional rhyme. Give each child a small treat (a pumpkin drawn on the back of the hand, a piece of pumpkin-shaped candy, a pumpkin sticker) when they have managed to do it.

Practice chanting this rhyme with children. After chanting is mastered, use different motions to keep a steady beat: clapping, snapping fingers, hitting thighs, tapping index fingers on noses, and so on.

Write the nursery rhyme on chart paper and point to each of the words with a pumpkin pointer as you read to reinforce left-to-right progression. Hot glue a small three-dimensional pumpkin to the end of a wooden dowel or use an orange paper pumpkin with a curl of green ribbon.

Write the rhyme on chart paper and laminate. Call out different letters or words and have individuals come up and circle them with a wipe-off marker. Start by having a student circle all the *Pp*'s in the rhyme. Count the number of *Pp*'s. On different days, work on other language conventions and phonics skills, such as circling words with long vowel sounds, contractions, periods and commas, and rhyming words.

Make a class lift-the-flap book. Have each child cut a pumpkin from orange construction paper. Help them cut windows in the pumpkins. Glue the orange pumpkins to white sheets of construction paper (careful not to glue the window shut!) and show children how to add a cutout green leaf and a green-marker tendril. Inside the pumpkin window, invite children to draw pictures of what they would keep in a pumpkin shell. Add the words, *(Child's name) would keep* _____ *in a pumpkin shell.* Display the pictures on a bulletin board or bind the pages together, adding a cover of pumpkins and a title page.

Jeremy would keep Batman in a pumpkin shell.

Make a pumpkin village. Cut three or four different-shaped pumpkins from tagboard (fat pumpkin, round pumpkin, tall pumpkin). The pumpkin shapes should be about as big as a large paper plate. Have children trace their chosen pumpkin shapes onto orange construction paper and then add windows, door, chimneys, and other details from construction paper scraps. Display the pumpkin houses side-by-side on a bulletin board with the title "Put Us in a Pumpkin Shell!"

 Children will especially enjoy reading the story *Peter's Pumpkin House* by Colin and Moira Maclean (Kingfisher Books, 1992). This is the story of Peter of pumpkin-eater fame, who is really a chimney sweep and lives in his pumpkin-shell house with his wife, Mrs. P., and their baby. They wake up one morning to find that someone has been nibbling on their house. As Peter looks all over the city, he finds nursery-rhyme characters using pumpkins in different ways (pumpkin soup, jack-o'- lanterns, heads for scarecrows, pumpkin pie). Finally Peter discovers that it's really a goat from Shoe Cottage nibbling away each night. This is an absolutely delightful story! Have children write other stories about Peter, his family, and other adventures in the pumpkin house in Nursery Rhyme Land.

 Look for different sizes of pumpkin-shaped cookie cutters to use with orange play dough. Children can use the cookie cutters to make Peter's house or they can form balls to make pumpkins.

 Look for Marcia Vaughn's simple book for emergent readers, *Knock Knock* (Celebration Press/Scott Foresman, 1996), which is a take-off on Peter and his house. Peter has a party and invites his friends—Humpty Dumpty, Bo Peep, Old King Cole, Little Boy Blue, and Miss Muffet. All of his friends come but are scared away by a spider!

Look for Joan Walsh Anglund's *In a Pumpkin Shell* (Harcourt Brace Jovanovich, 1960). The cover pictures an old lady reading stories outside of her pumpkin house. There is an illustrated nursery rhyme for each letter of the alphabet and of course, "Peter, Peter, Pumpkin Eater" is written and illustrated for the letter *P*. Show each page as you read the poem, asking children to identify the letter of the alphabet and guess the word from the illustration.

Have children brainstorm what a family of pumpkin people would look like. Perhaps they would have pumpkins for heads, pumpkins for bodies, and pumpkin-shaped shoes. After children have discussed the possibilities, have them draw or paint a pumpkin family (including a pumpkin-shaped pet!). Encourage more mature students to write or dictate stories about their pumpkin families.

Go to a pumpkin farm where you can pick your own pumpkins or to a farmer's market where children can choose a class pumpkin. Videotape the trip for the children to enjoy again and again. Choose a pumpkin that is large enough to cut into Peter's pumpkin house. Cut a round hole in the *bottom* and scoop out all the seeds and pulp. Save the seeds to dry and use in a pumpkin counting game (see below). Ask children if you should cut doors and windows, how many, where they should be cut, and how big they should be. Shave the cutout pieces to about half an inch in thickness and save them so that children can fit them back into the pumpkin house to close the doors and windows. Put the pumpkin on a low table and provide small toy people so that children can act out the rhyme of Peter and his wife.

When you have finished with your pumpkin house, put the pumpkin in your water table and give children pumpkin knives with which to cut the pieces into smaller pieces. Add some pumpkin scoops, ice cream scoops, heavy plastic knives, large spoons, and so on. Encourage children to cut the pumpkin up any way they like.

If you cannot get away for a field study, read to the class *The Pumpkin Patch* by Patricia Miles Martin (G. P. Putnam's Sons, 1966), which is the story of a class field trip to a pumpkin patch.

Put orange paint at the easel and remind children that pumpkins are roughly the shape of a circle. Encourage children to paint pumpkins. After the orange paint has dried, give children another color to use for painting details to make Peter's pumpkin house.

Make pumpkin-shaped flashcards. Write uppercase letters on pumpkin shapes cut from tagboard (or use sheets from pumpkin-shaped note pads) and leave the pumpkins out to encourage individual children to put the pumpkins in alphabetical order. When the children are proficient with uppercase letters, make a set of lowercase letters. For more mature students, flash the cards and ask the children to name the letter that comes next or to give a word that starts with the letter. Make pumpkin house flashcards to teach other concepts, too (numeral recognition, number words, sight words, color words).

Make a pumpkin lacing card by cutting a pumpkin shape from orange construction paper or use a sheet from a pumpkin-shaped note pad.

Add a door and windows for Peter's house. Mount on tagboard and laminate. Punch holes around the perimeter of the pumpkin and find a coordinating shoelace. Make a lacing card for each child to take home or one just for the class.

Write the letter *P* at the top of a piece of chart paper, a sheet cut in the shape of a pumpkin, or a commercially made pumpkin chart. Help children brainstorm all the words they can think of that start with the letter *P*. Add to the list as the week goes along.

Make dot-to-dot pumpkins using the numbers that children know. Write a number next to each dot and have children connect the dots with an orange crayon or marker. They can finish the pumpkin houses by adding details and coloring them. Leave out orange markers and white drawing paper to encourage children to make dot-to-dot pumpkins for each other.

Try a little pumpkin bingo. Make bingo cards in the shape of pumpkins. Use pumpkin-shaped candy, pumpkin seeds, or orange plastic bingo chips to cover cards. Practice whatever skill is appropriate for your class—colors, numerals, sight words, or lowercase letters.

Draw and cut out pumpkin shapes from orange construction paper and add doors and windows. Laminate for durability. Write a number on each pumpkin. Children use pumpkin seeds (or orange plastic bingo chips, pumpkin-shaped erasers, or orange pompoms) as counters to count the appropriate number of seeds onto each pumpkin.

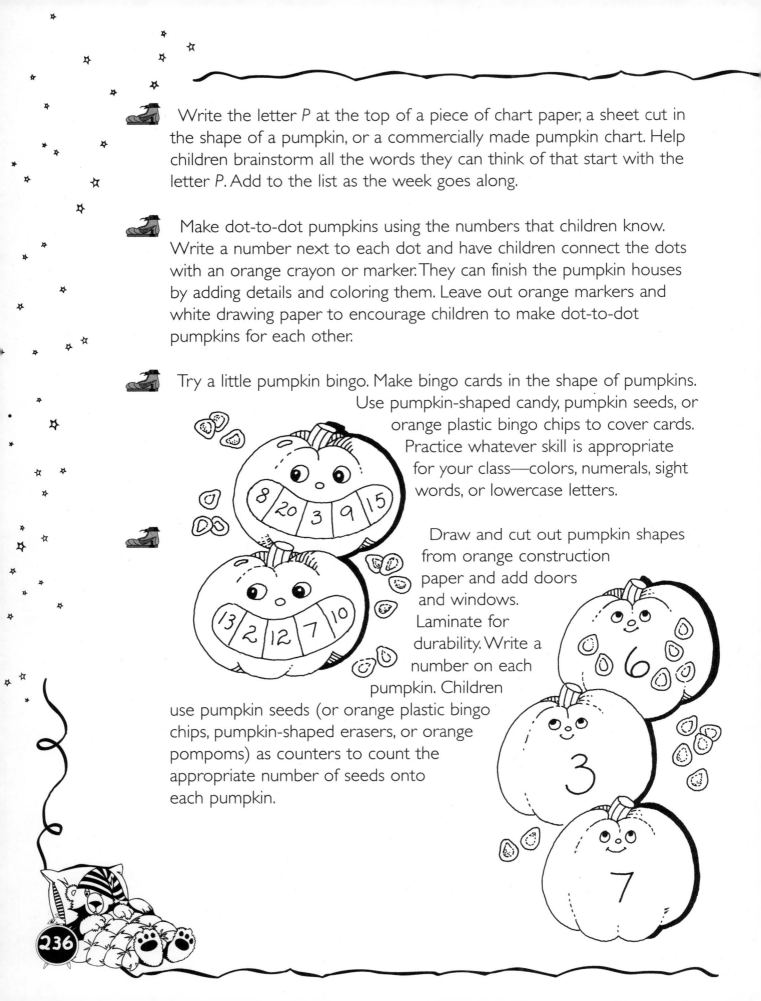

Enjoy some of these books that feature pumpkins. As you introduce each book, encourage children to predict what they think will happen from looking at the illustration on the front cover.

Adish, Roz. *The Pumpkin Heads*. Prentice Hall, 1968.

Benarde, Anita. *The Pumpkin Smasher*. Walker, 1972.

Berenstain, Stan and Jan. *The Berenstain Bears and the Prize Pumpkin*. Random House, 1990.

Berger, Melvin. *Growing Pumpkins*. Newbridge, 1993. (big book)

Cavagnaro, David. *The Pumpkin People*. Scribner's, 1979.

Dillon, Jana. *Jeb Scarecrow's Pumpkin Patch*. Houghton Mifflin, 1992.

Hall, Zoe. *It's Pumpkin Time!* Blue Sky Press, 1994.

Hellsing, Lennart. *The Wonderful Pumpkin*. Atheneum, 1976.

Johnston, Tony. *The Vanishing Pumpkin*. G. P. Putnam's Sons, 1983.

Kroll, Steven. *The Biggest Pumpkin Ever*. Holiday House, 1984.

Lexau, Joan. *The Big, Big Pumpkin*. Field Publications, 1985.

Luttrell, Ida. *Ottie Slockett*. Dial, 1990.

Martin, Patricia Miles. *The Pumpkin Patch*. G. P. Putnam's Sons, 1966.

McDonald, Megan. *The Great Pumpkin Switch*. Orchard Books, 1992.

Miller, Edna. *Mousekin's Golden House*. Treehouse, 1970.

Ray, M. L. *Pumpkins*. Harcourt Brace, 1992.

Ross, Katherine. *The Little Pumpkin Book*. Random House, 1992.

Somerville, Sheila. *Five Little Pumpkins*. Nellie Edge Resources, 1988.

Titherington, Jeanne. *Pumpkin Pumpkin*. Greenwillow Books, 1986.

Zagwyn, Deborah T. *Pumpkin Blanket*. Celestial Arts, 1991.

This is the house that Jack built.

This is the malt
that lay in the house that Jack built.

This is the rat
That ate the malt
that lay in the house that Jack built.

This is the cat that killed the rat
That ate the malt
that lay in the house that Jack built.

This is the dog
That worried the cat that killed the rat
That ate the malt
that lay in the house that Jack built.

This is the cow with the crumpled horn
That tossed the dog
That worried the cat that killed the rat

That ate the malt
that lay in the house that Jack built.

This is the maiden all forlorn
That milked the cow with the crumpled horn
That tossed the dog
That worried the cat that killed the rat
That ate the malt
that lay in the house that Jack built.

This is the man all tattered and torn
That kissed the maiden all forlorn
That milked the cow with the crumpled horn
That tossed the dog
That worried the cat that killed the rat
That ate the malt
that lay in the house that Jack built.

This is the parson all shaven and shorn
That married the man all tattered and torn
That kissed the maiden all forlorn
That milked the cow with the crumpled horn
That tossed the dog
That worried the cat that killed the rat
That ate the malt
that lay in the house that Jack built.

This is the cock that crowed in the morn
That woke the parson all shaven and shorn
That married the man all tattered and torn
That kissed the maiden all forlorn
That milked the cow with the crumpled horn
That tossed the dog
That worried the cat, that killed the rat
That ate the malt
that lay in the house that Jack built.

This is the farmer sowing his corn
That kept the cock that crowed in the morn
That woke the parson all shaven and shorn
That married the man all tattered and torn
That kissed the maiden all forlorn
That milked the cow with the crumpled horn
That tossed the dog
That worried the cat that killed the rat
That ate the malt
that lay in the house that Jack built.

More mature children will love this cumulative nursery rhyme. Look for one of the many books that illustrate the rhyme.

Adams, Pam. *This Is the House That Jack Built*. Child's Play, 1996.

Bolam, Emily. *The House That Jack Built*. Dutton, 1992.

Cooke, Donald. *This Is the House That Jack Built*. Holt, 1963.

Cutts, David. *The House That Jack Built*. Troll Associates, 1979.

Galdone, Paul. *The House That Jack Built*. McGraw-Hill, 1961.

Peppe, Rodney. *The House That Jack Built*. Delacorte Press, 1985.

Stevens, Janet. *The House That Jack Built*. Holiday House, 1985.

Stow, Jenny. *The House That Jack Built*. Dial Books for Young Readers, 1992.

One book of special notice that illustrates this rhyme is Elizabeth Falconer's *House That Jack Built* (Hambleton-Hill, 1994), which includes rebus pictures for each of the main words. Children will love "reading" this book with you—you read the words and then stop at each picture. The children "read" the picture.

Find a picture of this verse or use the illustration on page 238. Copy the picture or series of pictures and mount on a large piece of tagboard. Discuss what children see in the pictures. Help children identify each of the nouns in the rhyme. Draw a line from each noun out to the margin and write the word in the margin. Children may identify other things that do not relate directly to the rhyme, which is fine. Review pertinent vocabulary each day.

Set up a writing center under the labeled picture of the rhyme. Put out markers, pencils, crayons, and white paper. Encourage students to copy the words from the margin or draw pictures of the words.

Children will enjoy acting out this rhyme. Make your own line drawings, have children illustrate each character, or use the illustrations of the house, malt, rat, cat, dog, cow, maiden, man, parson, cock, and farmer on pages 268–272. Mount the pictures on tagboard and laminate. Punch holes on each side of the tagboard, attach string or yarn, and have children wear the pictures around their neck. Or make stick puppets for children to hold by gluing the pictures to craft sticks. Invite cast members to sit in order at the front of the room. As each cast member's line is said, he or she stands. Stand behind the players and tap each one on the shoulder in succession, if needed, until the entire rhyme is complete. The visual cues will help students learn the rhyme very quickly.

Another way to act out the rhyme is to use the props in the activity above and have each child memorize a part. This is a great way to present the rhyme for parents.

Make a class reproduction of the rhyme. Prewrite the words for each verse, one verse per page, on the bottoms of sheets of drawing paper. Invite volunteers to illustrate each verse. Hang the verses in order on a bulletin board. After children have enjoyed this display, bind the pages into a class book.

 Make a pocket-chart story by writing the main words from the rhyme on sentence strips.

the <u>farmer</u> sowing his corn	that kept
the <u>cock</u> that crowed in the morn	that woke
the <u>parson</u> all shaven and shorn	that married
the <u>man</u> all tattered and torn	that kissed
the <u>maiden</u> all forlorn	that milked
the <u>cow</u> with the crumpled horn	that tossed
the <u>dog</u>	that worried
the <u>cat</u>	that killed
the <u>rat</u>	that ate
the <u>malt</u>	that lay in
the <u>house</u>	that Jack built

Place the last sentence strip in the pocket chart first—at the bottom of the chart—for children to read. Then add the next sentence strip above the first one and read both lines, and so on. You are building a story from the bottom up. For children who do not "read," add illustrations on index cards at the end of each line. These visual clues will help children remember the words.

Write each of the underlined words on page 242 on a sentence strip and illustrate each on an index card. Use line drawings, children's illustrations, or the illustrations on pages 268–272. Put the word strips in a pocket chart or on the floor and have children find the matching picture. After children have had experience with matching pictures to the individual words, hold up each picture and have a student find the matching word in a chart of the rhyme.

 Make a "favorite part" graph. List all the characters in a column down the left side of a graph (on the chalkboard or chart paper). Give children index cards on which to draw their favorite characters. Invite children to attach their illustrations in rows next to the appropriate character. Discuss the results.

 Enjoy Joan Heilbroner's innovation *This Is the House Where Jack Lives* (Harper & Row, 1962) with the class. Encourage children to write their own innovations, such as "This Is the Book That Mother Goose Wrote," "This Is the Book That Our Class Wrote," "This Is the House Where I Live," or "This Is the School Where I Learn."

Read other cumulative rhymes to the children, such as "Twelve Days of Christmas," "There Was an Old Lady Who Swallowed a Fly," Audrey Wood's *The Napping House* (Harcourt Brace, 1989), or *The Napping House Woke Up* (Harcourt Brace, 1994). After you have read several of these, see if children can come up with their own definition of what a cumulative rhyme is. Reinforce any child who finds and identifies another cumulative rhyme during the year.

There was a crooked man and he walked a crooked mile;

He found a crooked sixpence upon a crooked stile;

He bought a crooked cat, which caught a crooked mouse;

And they all lived together in a crooked little house.

A traditional tune for this nursery rhyme can be found in Pamela Beall and Susan Nipp's *Wee Sing Nursery Rhymes and Lullabies* (Price, Stern & Sloan, 1985). The *Wee Sing* set comes with an audio cassette and sing-along book. It is easily found in most toy, book, or school-supply stores or can be ordered directly from Price, Stern & Sloan Publishers, Inc., 410 North La Cienega Boulevard, Los Angeles, CA 90048.

This rhyme uses some vocabulary that children may not be familiar with. Copy the illustration above and mount on tagboard. Help the class label the vocabulary in the picture—*man, sixpence* (the sum of six British pennies), *stile* (steps used for climbing over a fence), *cat, mouse,* and *house.* Draw lines out from the pictures and write the words in the margins. Children will find other things to label that do not relate directly to the poem, which is fine. Each day, review the words that

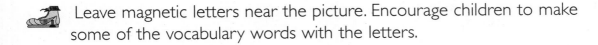

the class has identified, pointing out those that relate specifically to the rhyme.

Leave magnetic letters near the picture. Encourage children to make some of the vocabulary words with the letters.

Have each child illustrate the rhyme or any part of the rhyme—a crooked man with a crooked staff, a crooked road, a crooked house, and so on.

Write the entire rhyme on sentence strips and have children watch while you cut the sentence strips into individual words. Place the individual words in order in a pocket chart and read the rhyme together with the class. Have children close their eyes while one child comes up and turns a word over. Children open their eyes and guess the mystery word. Whoever guesses correctly takes the next turn.

After you have cut the rhyme into individual words, give the word cards out to students. Display the rhyme on chart paper and invite children to recreate each line by bringing the appropriate words to the front. Help children stand so that the words they are holding are in the correct order. Read the line together while the children are standing, then go to the next line. At the end, try putting the words in alphabetical order.

Write the rhyme on chart paper and laminate. Have individuals come up and mark selected words by drawing a crooked circle or a crooked square with wipe-off marker. On subsequent days, work on other language conventions and phonics skills, such as short vowel sounds, semicolons, or the word *crooked*.

Write the word *crooked* on sticky notes and have children match each sticky-note to an occurrence of the word *crooked* on the chart. Count the number of times children see the word *crooked*.

After children have worked with the laminated rhyme chart for several days, give each child a copy of the rhyme. Call out some of the same phonics skills and language conventions that you identified on the chart and have students find the same things on their individual sheets. For example, you might have them circle all the lowercase c's with a green crayon, underline all the capital letters with a red crayon, and make a crooked X in each space between words.

 Teach children to memorize this rhyme by echo. Say the first line of the rhyme and then have children echo it back to you. Say the next line and have them echo it back. Repeat until you have said and echoed the entire rhyme. Have a child who memorizes quickly be the leader and invite the class to echo back to that child. Or divide the class into two groups and have one group lead and the other echo.

Chant this rhyme with the children. After they have memorized and mastered chanting the rhyme, keep a steady beat by clapping hands, bending wrists up and down, snapping fingers, bending side-to-side at the waist, or any other motions you or the children can think of. Bring out your rhythm instruments. Divide children into four groups and give each one a different instrument. Have each group chant and beat one line of the rhyme. Point to each group when their turn comes.

Help children think of an innovation for this rhyme. Substitute a different word for *crooked*, such as a color.

> There was a blue man and he walked a blue mile;
>
> He found a blue sixpence upon a blue stile;
>
> He bought a blue cat, which caught a blue mouse;
>
> And they all lived together in a blue little house.

Use sticky notes to put new words over the words in the original rhyme on the laminated chart. Read each new rhyme with the class. Invite children to illustrate each innovation.

Make up sheets of crooked dotted lines for children to trace. After children have traced these lines, leave out markers and white paper so that children may make crooked lines for themselves and others to trace. Encourage each child to write his or her name with "crooked" letters.

House Activities

Record individuals and groups of children singing and reading the rhymes in this unit. Sprinkle in commercial recordings of the rhymes and place the audio cassette in the listening center. Children will enjoy listening to the class and hearing themselves on the tape.

Read books about strange houses, such as Susan Schade and Jon Bueller's *Snug House, Bug House* (Random House, 1994), which is about a group of bugs that make a house from a tennis ball. Show children pictures of each of the houses from the nursery rhymes: the shoe house, the pumpkin house, and the crooked house. Encourage children to design and draw strange houses that they would like to live in.

Make an ABC book of strange houses. Write the letters of the alphabet down the left side of a sheet of chart paper. With the class, brainstorm some strange house possibilities for each letter. For example, A—apple house, B—banana boat house, C—crooked house. Invite volunteers to illustrate each letter and bind the pages alphabetically into a class book.

With the children, brainstorm a list of things found in houses that children might count for homework (lamps, windows, doors, sinks, or pictures on walls). Have children make up a counting sheet to take home. Choose one item to graph when children return their sheets.

Send home a piece of tagboard with each child. Have children work with their families to design a house that looks like their own. When all the house projects are returned, display them side-by-side on a bulletin board with the title "Open House." If some children do not return the project, just put a sign that says, "Lot # ____ Under Construction."

Discuss with children all the building materials you have in the room that they might use to build houses: wooden blocks, plastic interlocking blocks, bristly blocks, 1-inch blocks, sand, or whatever you have available. Encourage each child to choose some type of building material and design a house. Reinforce creativity and imagination. Have an instant camera available and take a photograph of each child beside his or her masterpiece. Under each picture, write *This is the house that (child's name) built!* If you like, mount the photographs on tagboard and have children write or dictate a few sentences about their houses.

Help children think of verses and motions to the tune of "Here We Go 'Round the Mulberry Bush." For example

> This is the way we build our house, build our house, build our house.
>
> This is the way we build our house, so early in the morning.

Other verses might include sawing the wood, hammering the nails, painting the walls, and so on. Challenge children to make up some more verses with accompanying motions.

Brainstorm a list of materials that houses can be made of. Ask each child to name what type of house he or she lives in. Then read one of the following versions of the beloved fairy tale "The Three Little Pigs," pointing out the three types of houses that the little pigs built—straw, sticks, and bricks.

Bell, Sally. *Three Little Pigs.* Western, 1991.

Biro, Val. *Three Little Pigs.* Oxford University Press, 1991.

Bishop, Gavin. *Three Little Pigs.* Scholastic, 1990.

Blegvad, Erik. *Three Little Pigs.* Margaret K. McElderry Books, 1994.

Bucknall, Caroline. *Three Little Pigs.* Dial Books, 1987.

Ceccarelli, Serge. *Three Little Pigs.* Barron, 1988.

Galdone, Paul. *Three Little Pigs.* Ticknor & Fields, 1988.

Learn this traditional fingerplay with motions.

This is the roof of the house so good,   palms facing, fingertips touching

These are the walls made of wood.   palms facing, hands straight

This is the window that lets in light,   index fingers and thumbs touching, making a

square

This is the door that shuts so tight.   fingers and palms together

This is the chimney so straight and tall,   Raise one index finger.

What a good house for us, one and all!   Point to self on *one* and to children on *all*.

There are many types of houses that animals and people live in. See if children can tell you who lives in each of these: cocoon, hive, nest, igloo, tent, burrow, sty, egg, stall, palace, cage, aquarium, underground cave, hole. Can children think of more? Encourage them to read books to find out about some others.

Enjoy the big book *Where Do Animals Live?* by Melvin Berger (Newbridge, 1996) with its simple text and beautiful photographs.

Share some of the following books about houses with your class.

Ackerman, Karen. *This Old House.* Atheneum, 1992.

Bour, Daniel. *The House From Morning to Night.* Kane/Miller Book Publishers, 1985.

Brown, Marc, *There's No Place Like Home.* Parent's Magazine, 1984.

Brown, Richard. *100 Words About My House.* Harcourt Brace Jovanovich, 1988.

Donaldson, Julia. *A Squash and a Squeeze.* Margaret K. McElderry Books, 1993.

Dorros, Arthur. *This Is My House.* Scholastic, 1992.

Gibbons, Gail. *How a House Is Built.* Holiday House, 1990.

Gold, Kari Jenson. *A World of Homes.* Newbridge, 1996. (big book and/or student six-pack)

Hoberman, Mary. *A House Is a House for Me.* Viking Press, 1978.

Jensen, Patricia. *My House.* Childrens Press, 1990.

Kalman, Bobbie. *Homes Around the World.* Crabtree Publishing, 1994.

LeSieg, Theodore. *In a People House.* Random House, 1972.

Morris, Ann. *Houses and Homes.* Lothrop, Lee & Shepard, 1992.

Roffey, Maureen and Bernard Lodge. *Door to Door: A Split Page Picture Book.* Whispering Coyote Press, 1993.

Williams, Rozanne Lanczak. *Who Lives Here?* Creative Teaching Press, 1994.

Zelinsky, Paul O. *The Maid and the Mouse and the Odd-Shaped House.* Dutton Children's Books, 1981.

Wrapping It Up
Culminating Activities

Nursery-Rhyme Center

Set up a nursery-rhyme center in your classroom. Provide a trunk of costume pieces (king and queen crowns, robes, sunglasses, mittens, mouse and cat ears and tails), and a box of props (plastic spider or spider puppet, pie tins, staff, plastic eggs, stick horses, sand pail, plastic pumpkin, bowls, spoons, bubble pipe). Add any props or costumes used as you study each new rhyme. Provide a stage area and an audience area. Encourage children to use the props both to act out the rhymes and to make up new ones!

Charades

Choose a child to come and whisper a rhyme in your ear. Then have the child choose students to act out the rhyme. Send those children to a corner of the room and have them practice pantomiming the chosen rhyme. Repeat with another child until each child is involved with a group. Set a time limit and then have each group come back and perform their rhyme for the class to guess.

Favorite Rhymes Graph

Have each child draw a picture of his or her favorite rhyme on a small unlined index card. Write the names of the rhymes across the bottom of the chalkboard and invite children to place their pictures above the appropriate names of the rhymes on the graph. Discuss the results. On another day, have children draw favorite nursery-rhyme characters to graph and discuss.

Picture Clues

Have several collections of nursery rhymes at your book center. Each day, choose a different collection. Turn the pages and ask the class, "Do you know this rhyme?" If someone guesses the rhyme from the pictures, they get to lead the class in saying the rhyme. If no one knows it, just skip that page and go to the next.

Recitations

Have each child choose a favorite nursery rhyme to recite for the rest of the class. Choose a place "onstage"(on top of a set of steps or on top of a low table). Introduce each child with some fanfare and then have the child recite the rhyme and bow to the audience. Lead the audience in grateful applause after each recitation.

Nursery Rhyme Character Parade

Tell parents ahead of time that you will be parading for the school. Encourage parents to work with their children to decide on favorite nursery-rhyme characters and create costumes to wear for the day. Encourage parents to make creative use of what they already have at home. Walk with children through the halls of your school or through some selected classrooms. After the parade, ask children why they chose the particular characters they did.

Nursery-Rhyme Bingo

To make your own nursery-rhyme bingo game, select a picture clue for each nursery rhyme you have studied. Photocopy the clues, then cut and paste to make individual bingo cards. Make a set of master cards with the same pictures for the caller. First the caller turns over a card and shows it to the class. Then the children name the rhyme, recite it, and cover it on their cards if they can. The game continues until someone covers an entire card. That person gets to be the caller and the game starts again.

Nursery-Rhyme Memorization

Get families involved in helping children practice nursery rhymes at home. Send the words home (in case parents have forgotten them!) and include the following slip. Each time a child returns a slip, he or she gets a special treat, such as a nursery-rhyme sticker. Parents are your best partners!

_____
(child's name)

has memorized _____!
(name of rhyme)

_____
Signature of Parent or Guardian

_____
Date

Name That Tune

Use any commercial audio cassette or record of traditional nursery rhyme tunes. Play the first few bars of the song or rhyme and challenge children to name that tune. If they can't, play a little more until they can. When the rhyme is identified, have the class recite or sing the rhyme along with the tape.

Class Audio Cassette

Record both individual children and the class singing or reciting each nursery rhyme. Put the tape in your listening center. Ask parents who'd like copies to send in blank cassettes, then find a parent who has the equipment to make copies for others. Encourage parents to listen to the tape with their children in the car, before bed, and whenever else they can stand it!

Class Nursery-Rhyme Collection

Take a photograph of the actors each time the class acts out a nursery rhyme. Buy a scrapbook with clear sheets over each page. At the bottom of each page, write the title of the nursery rhyme—put the photographs at the top. Children will look at this book and read the rhymes again and again.

Individual Nursery-Rhyme Collections

Show and discuss several nursery-rhyme collections with children. Explain that the illustrator usually chooses favorite rhymes and then interprets them in pictures. Encourage children to make their own collections by preparing pages for all the rhymes that you teach with the words at the bottom. Encourage children to take their favorites and illustrate the rhymes at the top of each page. Bind each collection together and have children design a cover, title page, dedication page, and an "About the Author" page.

Mother Goose Scavenger Hunt

Tell children that Mother Goose has left them a surprise and that they must follow some clues to find it. Invite staff members all over the school to get involved. Start the hunt with a clue written on a card. For example, *Go to the secretary's office and find the thing that scared Miss Muffet.* Each mystery item will produce a clue when children find it. For instance, when children get to the secretary's office, a plastic spider will be sitting on a new clue card. The clues continue, taking the class on a tour of the school, with the final clue leading to a snack—queen's tarts, Peter's pumpkin muffins, or three kitten's pie.

Nursery-Rhyme Video

Keep a video camera in your room and film the children as you work through the unit. Presentations are nice, such as children acting out "Humpty Dumpty," but catch the simpler things, too—a child putting together a nursery rhyme puzzle, telling a nursery rhyme with flannel-board pieces, singing a song with handmade hats, cutting a real pumpkin for Peter's pumpkin house. Children will watch this video over and over (great reinforcement of the rhymes!) or you can send it home with a different child each night! Invite parents in for a nursery-rhyme tea and show the video (videos can be edited!) as the major attraction. What a wonderful gift and keepsake of their year with you for children and parents!

Resources

Favorite Collections

There are over 140 nursery-rhyme collections in print. Below is a sampling of some of the children's favorites. Do not limit yourself to this list—check your local library for these and others.

Animal Crackers by Jane Dyer. Little, Brown, 1996.

This collection includes classic nursery rhymes and more. With its beautiful oversize illustrations, it will be a favorite.

Animal Nursery Rhymes selected by Angela Wilkes. Dorling Kindersley, 1992.

This collection includes real animals and real children dressed up in costumes to illustrate each rhyme. It is a wonderful collection to have on hand throughout your study so that children can look up what the real animals look like. It will give you ideas for costumes, too. There's simply nothing else like it.

Cyndy Szekeres' Favorite Mother Goose Rhymes. Golden Books, 1992.

This collection includes favorite, classic rhymes with nice illustrations.

Hey Diddle Diddle and Other Mother Goose Rhymes: A Lift-the-Flap Book by Shoo Rayner. Puffin, 1995.

This is a must-have for the youngest listener. Lifting the flaps holds wonder for young children. This short collection includes nine of the more popular nursery rhymes.

James Marshall's Mother Goose by James Marshall. Farrar, Straus, & Giroux, 1979.

This collection includes verses that appeal to Marshall's own sense of humor. Some are favorites and some are not as well-known, but the illustrations are fresh and funny and will appeal to children . . . and adults!

Mother Goose: A Sampler. Douglas and McIntyre/Groundwood Books, 1994.

This Canadian collection is called a sampler because different artists were asked to illustrate each rhyme—a unique visual experience!

Mother Goose's Little Misfortunes by Leonard S. Marcus and Amy Schwartz. Bradbury, 1990.

Marcus has taken 18 Mother Goose rhymes and added little misfortunes. Both the rhymes and Schwartz's illustrations are humorous.

Mother Goose's Words of Wit and Wisdom: A Book of Months. Dial, 1990.

You will love the beautiful and unusual illustrations of this collection. Tedd Arnold's designs were cross-stitched and then photographed to illustrate each of the rhymes.

Mother Hubbard's Surprise Book by Laura Rader. Tambourine Books, 1993.

This collection illustrates some of the most familiar rhymes. What makes it interesting and different is the split page on every other page. A unique and fun collection.

My Very First Mother Goose edited by Iona Opie, illustrated by Rosemary Wells. Candlewick Press, 1996.

This is a large book with a different slant on some favorite verses. The illustrations are wonderful. It is an excellent collection and is a good one to suggest to parents for their own libraries.

Nick Butterworth's Book of Nursery Rhymes. Viking, 1990.

The humor in this collection is in the illustrations. You'll love the mouse pole-vaulting over a candlestick!

Pudding and Pie by Sara Williams. Oxford University, 1989.

This collection of 40 nursery rhymes includes an audio cassette with inspired musical arrangements.

William Wegman's Mother Goose. Hyperion, 1996.

This wonderfully humorous collection contains all the favorite rhymes, but each rhyme uses real dogs as the main characters. This is a funny collection for children who are familiar with the more traditional illustrations.

Rebus Collections

These are collections of nursery rhymes that include pictures for many of the key words. Such collections provide ideas for which words to replace with pictures. You might even want to include a rebus copy of the rhyme at the end of each class book you make. Children will also simply enjoy "reading" these rhymes.

Mother Goose Picture Rhymes illustrated by Andrew Geeson. Derrydale Books, 1994.

The Rebus Treasury compiled by Jean Marzollo. Dial Books for Young Readers, 1986.

Collections With Special Groups in Mind

Because nursery rhymes are so popular, many collections have been selected with special groups in mind. This list is not all-inclusive but may be of interest to specific groups or those with special interests.

Black Mother Goose by Elizabeth Murphy-Oliver. Dare Books, 1981.

Chinese Mother Goose compiled by Robert Wyndham. Putnam, 1982.

Christian Mother Goose Big Book by Marjorie Decker. World Bible, 1992.

Dragon Kites and Dragonflies: A Collection of Chinese Nursery Rhymes by Demi. Harcourt Brace, 1986.

Mother Goose Rhymes for Jewish Children by Sara G. Levy. Bloch, 1979.

Nightfeathers: Black Goose Rhymes by Sundaira Morninghouse. Open Hand Publishers, 1989.

Nursery Rhymes from Mother Goose: Told in Signed English by Harry
Bornstein and Karen L Saulnier. Kendall Green Publications, 1992.

Putting a Positive Twist to Old Rhymes

After learning the original rhymes, children will really enjoy these
collections of adaptations that put a positive twist on old favorites.
Chances are children will still prefer the older versions, but they will
appreciate these newer innovations, too.

Positively Mother Goose by Diane Loomans, et al. Starseed Press, 1991.
Gorgeous illustrations make this collection a treasure.

New Adventures of Mother Goose: Gentle Rhymes for Happy Times by
Bruce Lansky. Meadowbrook, 1993.

Nursery Rhymes: The Equal Rhyme Amendment by Father Gander.
Advocacy Press, 1995.

Nurture Rhymes and Sleepy Songs by Ken Hayes. Newport, 1994.

Music

There are many, many audio cassettes and records of nursery rhymes.
Throughout this text, *Wee Sing Nursery Rhymes and Lullabies* has been
recommended because it is a comprehensive collection (77 classic
nursery rhymes and lullabies) that includes an audio cassette, sheet
music, words, and additional verses to most of the rhymes. It uses the
traditional words and tunes. Look for other musical collections from
Disney; Barney; Hap Palmer; Sharon, Lois and Bram; and more.

One modern, upbeat collection of note is *Rhymin' to the Beat* by Jack
Hartman and Company (Hop 2 It Music, P.O. Box 28241, St.
Petersburg, FL 33709). This wonderful collection of nursery rhymes will
be enjoyed by children *after* they have mastered the traditional rhymes
and tunes.

Play nursery rhymes during "choice" times, and invite children to dance
to the music, play rhythm instruments to a steady beat, and march to

the music. Encourage parents to send in their own nursery-rhyme tapes and records to offer variety to the children.

Illustrating the Rhymes

Flannel Board

There are several sets of nursery-rhyme pieces for the flannel board sold by most major school supply companies. One wonderful set comes from Little Folk Felts (1601 Ottawa Road, Clearwater, FL 34616, 1-813-442-9953). This company prints directly onto the felt. The colors are beautiful and extremely durable for little hands. The pieces can even be washed! Don't just use flannel pieces on the flannel board—use your imagination and you will think of other ways to use the pieces that will help justify their cost.

You can, of course, make your own flannel-board pieces by cutting felt of different colors into shapes to represent the major parts of any of the rhymes. For instance, for "Jack and Jill," use green felt cut in the shape of a hill, a blue felt boy shape, a pink felt girl shape, and a yellow felt pail shape. There are also several suggestions throughout this text for taking the major players of any rhyme and assigning representational shapes (squares, circles, triangles) to represent the rhyme (see "Old King Cole," page 79). The simplicity of cutting shapes helps make the flannel board a daily part of your unit.

Cling pieces

Magnetic Way (division of Creative Edge, Inc., 2495 N. Forest Road, Amherst, NY 14069) makes sets of visual overlays that cling to glass, mirrors, and the Magnetic Way board. The Nursery Rhymes packet illustrates most of the rhymes in this book. The pieces can be used to illustrate the rhyme as you teach it or can be left out for children to manipulate as they say the rhymes themselves.

Puzzles

Wooden jigsaw puzzles

Wooden jigsaw puzzles are a staple in every early childhood classroom. Invest in some nursery rhyme puzzles. The best selection comes from Judy/Instructo. Instead of putting out a large assortment of puzzles on a rack, consider putting out just the puzzles that go with the rhymes you will be teaching that week and challenging students to do each puzzle independently within three minutes. Put a chart and an egg timer by the puzzle table. One child works the puzzle while another is the "verifier," who sets the timer, makes sure the child dumps all the pieces out, and makes sure the child puts them all back correctly before the timer dings! Each child who completes the puzzle within the time limit gets to add a sticker or stamp with his or her name on it to the chart. Evaluate the chart at the end of each week to see who is having trouble with puzzles!

Floor puzzles

Invest in a nursery-rhyme floor puzzle for more mature students. Encourage cooperative learning by having students do the puzzle in pairs. After students have had opportunities to work with the puzzle, encourage them to work the puzzle independently. Offer nursery-rhyme stickers to children who can put the puzzle together all by themselves.

Nursery-Rhyme Charts

Look for commercial charts that include nursery rhymes and colorful illustrations—one rhyme to a chart. There are charts available for most nursery rhymes—unfortunately, not all from the same company.

You do not have to buy commercial charts. You can write the words on chart paper and illustrate rhymes by enlarging and coloring the illustrations included in this book. Make sure to laminate commercial or handmade charts so that children can use markers to work on phonics skills and language conventions.

Nursery-Rhyme Stickers

There are many nursery-rhyme sticker sets. Use these in any number of ways.

★ Make your own nursery rhyme bingo game.

★ Make a sorting game with index cards. Place two stickers (some matching, some not) on each index card and have children sort the cards into stacks—cards with matching stickers and cards with different stickers.

★ Put three stickers on each index card, two alike and one different, and have students point to the two that are the same or the one that is different.

★ Use stickers as reinforcement for completing puzzles, memorizing rhymes, and so on.

★ Put one sticker on each index card. Place the index cards face down in front of the class and have one student come up and choose a card and turn it over. The class recites the rhyme that the sticker represents. A great "filler."

★ Have each child come up at the end of the day and choose a sticker, identify it, and say the rhyme.

★ Make a deck of playing cards using pairs of stickers and index cards. Use the cards to play go fish or concentration.

★ Make a lotto game by putting one set of stickers on a sheet of tagboard and a matching set of stickers on individual cards. Students match the cards to the stickers on the tagboard.

Videos

You will find several videos based on nursery rhymes. Children will especially enjoy the following after they have learned the rhymes.

"Mother Goose Stories: Jim Henson Preschool Collection." Buena Vista Home Video, 1995. 30 minutes each, several volumes.

"Barney Rhymes With Mother Goose." Lyons Group, 1992. 30 minutes.

"Richard Scarry's Best Sing-Along Mother Goose Video Ever!" Random House Home Video, 1994. 30 minutes.

"King Cole's Party." Price, Stern & Sloan, 1987. 55 minutes.

Thematic Links by Title

Baa Baa Black Sheep	Farm, Easter, Spring, Colors
Hey Diddle Diddle	Musical Instruments, Night Sky
Hickory Dickory Dock	Telling Time
Humpty Dumpty	Safety, Science (Eggs), Easter, Spring
I See the Moon	Night Sky, Five Senses (Sight)
It's Raining, It's Pouring	Weather, Spring (April Showers)
Itsy Bitsy Spider	Creepy Crawlies, Halloween, Spring
Jack and Jill	Science (Water), Concepts (Up and Down)
Little Bo Peep	Farm, Easter, Spring, Responsibility
Little Boy Blue	Farm, Musical Instruments, Colors, Responsibility
Little Jack Horner	Christmas, Fruit, Community Helpers (Bakery)
Little Miss Muffet	Creepy Crawlies, Halloween
Mary Had a Little Lamb	Farm, Pets, Community Helpers (School)
Old King Cole	Musical Instruments
Once I Caught a Fish Alive	Ocean, Streams and Lakes, Pond Life
1,2, Buckle My Shoe	Counting
1,2,3,4, Mary's at the Kitchen Door	Counting, Fruit
Pat-a-Cake	Community Helpers (Bakery)
Pease Porridge	Concepts (Hot and Cold), Science (Observation)

Peter Peter Pumpkin Eater	Pumpkins, Halloween, Thanksgiving, Colors
Pussycat, Pussycat	Pets
Queen of Hearts	Valentine's Day, Bakery, Honesty
Rain, Rain, Go Away	Weather, Spring (April Showers)
Rub-a-dub-dub	Community Helpers
Star Light, Star Bright	Night Sky, Shapes
Sing a Song of Sixpence	Birds, Colors, Community Helpers (Bakery), Counting
The House That Jack Built	Community Helpers (Carpenter)
There Was a Crooked Man	Drawing Lines
There Was an Old Woman	Tying Shoes, Families
This Old Man	Counting, Body Parts
Three Blind Mice	Five Senses
Three Little Kittens	Families, Winter (Mittens)
Twinkle Twinkle Little Star	Night Sky, Shapes

Thematic Links by Theme

Birds

Sing a Song of Sixpence

Christmas

Little Jack Horner

Colors

Baa Baa Black Sheep

Little Boy Blue

Peter Peter Pumpkin Eater

Sing a Song of Sixpence

Community Helpers

The House That Jack Built (Carpenter)

Little Jack Horner (Baker)

Mary Had a Little Lamb (Teacher)

Pat-a-Cake (Baker)

The Queen of Hearts (Baker)

Rub-a-dub-dub (Butcher, Baker, Candlestick Maker)

Sing a Song of Sixpence (Baker)

Concepts

Hey, Diddle Diddle (Over)

Jack and Jill (Up and Down)

Pease Porridge (Hot and Cold)

Counting

1,2, Buckle My Shoe

1,2,3,4, Mary's at the Kitchen Door

This Old Man

Creepy Crawlies

Itsy Bitsy Spider

Little Miss Muffet

Easter
Baa Baa Black Sheep
Humpty Dumpty
Little Bo Peep

Families
There Was an Old Woman
Three Little Kittens

Farm
Baa Baa Black Sheep
Little Bo Peep
Little Boy Blue
Mary Had a Little Lamb

Five Senses
I See the Moon
Three Blind Mice

Fruit
Little Jack Horner

Halloween
Itsy Bitsy Spider
Little Miss Muffet
Peter Peter Pumpkin Eater

Musical Instruments
Hey, Diddle Diddle
Little Boy Blue
Old King Cole

Pets
Mary Had a Little Lamb
Pussycat, Pussycat

Science
Humpty Dumpty (Eggs)
Jack and Jill (Water)
Once I Caught a Fish (Oceans,
    Streams and Lakes, Pond Life)

Shapes
Queen of Hearts
Star Light, Star Bright
Twinkle Twinkle Little Star

Spring
Baa Baa Black Sheep
Humpty Dumpty
It's Raining, It's Pouring
Itsy Bitsy Spider
Little Bo Peep
Little Miss Muffet
Rain, Rain, Go Away

Telling Time
Hickory Dickory Dock

Thanksgiving
Peter Peter Pumpkin Eater

Valentine's Day
Queen of Hearts

Weather
It's Raining, It's Pouring
Rain, Rain, Go Away

Winter
Three Little Kittens

Clip Art Index

271